Smith County, Tennessee

❧

Minute Book

1799-1804 & 1835

WPA Records
1936

Southern Historical Press, Inc.
PO Box 1267
Greenville, SC   29602

Please Direct All Correspondence and Book Orders to:
Southern Historical Press, Inc.
PO Box 1267
375 West Broad Street
Greenville, SC 29602-1267
or
southernhistoricalpress@gmail.com

ISBN #0-89308-332-1

W.P.A. RECORDS

The WPA Records are, for the most part, carbon copies of the original that was typed on onion skin paper during the Depression. Since these records were typed on poor machines by people who did not type in some cases and at the same time, they were read by persons not always sure of the older handwritten materials, the results are often less than perfect.

We have made every attempt to make as clear a copy as can be made from these older papers. Sometimes there are water stains and burned edges around the paper. This is the results of a fire at the home of one of the workers, Mrs. Penelope Allen, who was over most of the project. Sometimes, the index will be misleading in that they index by the middle name when a list of names are given in one family, i.e. "... the children of John Smith are, John, Jr., Mary Warren, and Oscar Sims. The indexer would list a Warren and a Sims in the index, when they should be Smith. Mountain Press has acquired a rather large number of finished and un-finished manuscripts. Many of these latter manuscripts are being typed and index now.

The WPA Records are now very scattered between the Tennessee State Library, various Public and Private Libraries and other collections. Some day, there is a hope that all of these can be collected and stored in one place. In spite of their many mistakes and problems, these are still the most complete collection of Tennessee records found anywhere.

SMITH COUNTY MINUTE BOOK
1799-1804 & 1835

P 1   State of Tennessee Smith County December 16th 1799 - Then the following
persons: Viz, Garrett Fitsgerald, William Alexander, James Gwin, Tilman Dixon,
Thomas Harneon, James Hibbits and Peter Turney Esquires being convened at the
dwelling house of the said Tilman Dixon; publickly took the Oath to support Constitution of the United States of America. Also the oath to support the Constitution of the State of Tennessee als the Oath of Office which is prescribed by
the law to be take by a Justice of the Peace and a Justice of the County Court
of Pleas and Quarter Sessions which several oaths were administered to the above
persons by Moses Fisk. After which the same oaths were administered to the said
Moses Fisk by the said Garrett Fitsgerald. Then by the unanimous vote of the
said Justices thus in Court Assembled the said Garrett Fitsgerald Esquire was
chosen Chairman of the said County Court of Pleas & Quarter Sessions for the said
County of Smith.

        Moses Fisk was then appointed Clerk pro tempre.

        William Walton Esquire then come into Court and the Oaths before mentioned
were administered to him to him by the Chairman.

        Amos Lacy was then appointed Constable protempore.

        The Court then adjourned till the Tuesday ensuing to meet at ten oolock in
the same place.

        Tuesday December the 17th 1799 The Court met according to adjournment, and
proceeded to appoint Sampson Williams to be Clerk of said Court John Martin
Sheriff of Smith County & Charles F. Mobias (Mabias) Coroner of said County.

        The said Sampson Williams then entered into bond with Tilman Dixon and
Garrett Fitsgerald his securities in the penal sum of ten thousand dollars for
the faithful discharge of the duties of his Office. And also took the Oath of
Office in open Court.

        Letter of attorney Elizabeth Young to William Marchbanks proven by the oath
of John Young one of the subscribing witnesses thereto.

        Letter of Attorney James Bradley to James Saunders acknowledged. James Gwinn
P 2   appointed County Trustee who give bond and security in the sum of two thousand
dollars, with Peter Turney, Richard Brittain and Elisha his securities. And took
the necessary oaths and the oath of Office.

        Charles F. Mobias came into Court and gave bond in the penal sum of five hundred
dollars, with William Saunders, and Henry McKinney his securities and also took the
necessary oaths and the oath of office.

        John Martin Sheriff came into Court and gave bond in the penal sum of five
thousand dollars with William Martin, Sampson Williams, and Grant Allen, his securities and also took the necessary oaths & the Oath of Office.

        The Court then proceeded to appoint a States Attorney and appointed Benjamin
Seawell who was duly quallified in open Court.

        The Court then proceeded to appoint a Register when Daniel Burford was duly
elected, gave bond in the penal sum of two thousand dollars with William Saunders
& William Martin his securities and also took the necessary oaths.

The Court then proceeded to Elect Constables, when Amos Lacy, Silas Jonakin, Robert Cotton, James Strain, James Wright and William Livingston, also Henry Huddleston.

The Court then proceeded to the appointment of Ranger, when Bazel Shaw was duly Elected. He then took the necessary oaths.

Court then adjourned until tomorrow morning eight oclock.

Wednesday December the 18th 1799 Court met according to adjournment. And the following members were present (to-wit) Garrett Fitsgerald, William Alexander, William Walton, James Gwinn, Tilman Dixon, Moses Fisk, James Hibbitts, Thomas Harmand and Peter Turney.

James Shaw came into Court and gave bond in the sum of five hundred dollars for the performance of his duty as Constable with James Gwinn his security took the necessary oaths & the oath of office.

Amos Lacey, Silas Jernigan, James W. Wright, all gave bond & security and took the necessary oaths and an oath of office as Constable.

P 3   On motion of Tilman Dixon ordered that all Tavern keepers be allowed to sell spirituous Liquors at the following rates (to wit) good whiskey and brandy 12½ cents by the half pint, For Breakfast, Dinner and Supper twenty five cents. For corn and oats by the gallon twelve & a half cents. For two Bundles of Fodder two pence, for pasturage 24 hours twelve & a half cents. For Lodging 6¼ cents.

Ordered that Tilman Dixon be allowed a Licence to keep Tavern he therefore gave bond with sufficient security.

A Letter of Attorney Tilman Dixon to Thomas Allen acknowledged.

On petition of Edmund Jennings Ordered that the said Edmund Jennings be allowed a ferry near the mouth of Jennings Creek who gave bond & security and allowed him the following rates (To wit) for man and horse 18 1/3 cents for single man & single Horse 9 cents for a waggon and team one dollar 25 cents cattle 6¼ for each head of hogs & sheep 6¼ and for pack horses the same as man & Horse.

Ordered that Henry McKinney be appointed overseer of the Road leading from Fort Blount to the head of Flins Creek from the south bank of Cumberland River and that all the hands living on Flins Creek waters and within three miles of said Road on the south side of the River work on said Road.

Ordered that William Saunders be appointed overseer of the Road leading from Paytons Creek to bledsoesborough & from thence to John Shelton's And that all his own hands together with James Braly (Bradley?) hands and Grant Allens hands all the hands living above Bledsoesborough between said Road and the River and below Paytons Creek work on said road.

The Court then proceeded to the appointment of of a Venire for the ensuing County Court when the following Gentlemen were appointed (To wit) John Keer (Kerr), John Bass, Daniel Mungle Andrew Greer John Brayard James Bradley, James Ballow, P 4   Anthony Samuel, William Lacy, Wm Kelton, Willeroy Pate, Pleasant Kearby, Grant Allen, William Martin Leonard Ballow, James Roberts, William Saunders, William Boyd, Thomas Bowman, Thomas Jamison, John Barclay, Henry Tooley, Nathaniel Ridley, William Haney, John Crosswhite, James Draper.

Ordered that Samuel Coruthers be appointed overseer of a Road leading from Mungles gap up the middle fork of Goose Creek to the first fork above the trough Spring.

5

Ordered that Elisha Oglesby be appointed overseer of a Road leading from the first fork of Goose Creek above the trough spring to Long Creek and down the same to the last crossing thereof and that James Gwin and James Hibbitts be appointed to give said overseers a list of polls to work on said Roads.

Ordered that William Gillispie be appointed overseer of a road from the last crossing of Long Creek to the State line & that the said James Gwin, James Hibits be appointed to give said overseer a list of hands to work on said road.

Ordered William Gilbreath be be appointed overseer of a Road leading from Cap Turneys to Mungles Gap. And that Tilman Dixon and Peter Turney be appointed to furnish a list of hands to work on s'd Road.

Robert Cotton who was appointed Constable came into Court & gave bond in the sum of five hundred dollars with Wm Alexander and Laurence Cotton his security and took the necessary oaths and the oath of office.

Edmund Jinnings stock mark recorded, a crop off the right ear, and an under bit of the left ear.

On motion of Major Dixon & Peter Turney to discontinue the Road leading from
P 5 said Turneys to Mungles or the Road leading from Dixons Springs to said Gap whereupon the Court determined to keep them open and and appointed overseers.

Ordered that Fredrick Debo be appointed overseer of the Road leading from Dixon Springs to Mungles Gap. and that John Shelton be appointed overseer of the Road leading from said Turney's by Dixons Springs to the Sumner line, along the old road and that Maj. Dixon & Cap Turney be appointed to divide the hands & give lists to the Overseer of the old road, and to be allowed toward the other two each 8 hands or that proportion should there be more or less hands liable to work on said Road.

Ordered that William Cochran be appointed Overseer of the Road leading from Dixons Springs, to Robert Bowmans, the hands who usually worked worked on said road to work as usual except those allotted to Captain Saunders.

Ordered that William Walton be appointed Overseer of the road leading from Paytons Creek to Walton Ferry that all the hands living below thomas Clarks on Payton's Creek and all the said creek within the first bend of the River above the to work on said Road.

Ordered that William Walton be appointed Overseer of the Road leading from the mouth of Caney fork to the head of Snow Creek and that his own hands together with all those living above said fork and below Sullivans Ferry to the head of Snow Creek to work on said Road.

Court then adjourned until the third Monday in March next.
Teste   Garret Fitzgerald,
Sampson Williams   William Alexander,
                                         James Gwinn.

Dixon Springs March 17th 1800 Court met according to adjournment when the following Gentlemen were present (To wit)   William Walton,
P 6   Thomas Harmand,
                                          James Hibits and
                                          Peter Turney Esquires.

The Court then proceeded to business and ordered that John Shelton be allowed to keep an ordinary at his own house als that David Cochran, be allowed to keep an

Ordinary at his now dwelling house and that they be rated agreeable to an order of last Court.

Deed William Saunders, to David Choohran Acknowledged.

Charles Hudspeth Esquire, appeared qualified & took his seat.

Ordered that Martha Aceff(Acuff) & John Aceff be allowed to administer on the Estate of Kean Acuff Deceasd.they having given bond & security and took the oath of Administrators. and also returned an Inventory into this Court.

Ordered that the late order of this Court be rescinded appointing John Shelton overseer of the Road from Peter Turny's to the Summer line and that the said John Shelton be reappointed overseer from the Summer County line to Dixons Lick Creek, and that Silas Jernigan be appointed overseer of said Road, from Lick Creek to said Turny's.

Ordered that the Grand Jury be impanelled & sworn when the following Gentlemen were elected & sworn: Viz: Grant Allen foreman, Willis Haney, John Barkley, Andrew Greer, Leonard Ballow, James Bradley, James Draper, Willeroy Pate, Anthony Samuel, James Ballow, William Kelton, Daniel Mungle, John Crosswhite, Thomas Jemison and Nathaniel Ridley.

Ordered that Amos Lacy be appointed to wate on the Grand Jury.

Ordered that Tandy Wither(Witcher) be appointed Constable who was accordingly Elected and gave security according to law.

Ordered that Henry Huddleston be appointed Constable who was accordingly Elected, & sworn & gave security according to law.

Ordered that Henry Tooley be excepted from serving as a Juror at this Term, also that Wm. Saunders be excepted from serving as a Juror at this term.

P 7   Ordered that a Jury be appointed to view, mark and lay off a road agreeable to law from Dixons Springs to the mouth of White Oak Creek by way James Gwins and that the following & that the following Gentlemen be appointed as Jurors: Viz: William Martin, James Hibbits, James Gwin, John Fisher, Robert Looney & John Bravard. and report the same to our ensuing Court.

Ordered that Sampson Williams Andrew Greer, Wilson Cage and Charles F. Mabias be appointed Juror to the Superior Court.

Ordered that Garret Fitsgerald be appointed to take in a list of the Taxable property for the Flins Creek Malitia Company. Charles Hudspeth Esquire for the Obeds River & Roaring river Company in Settlement William Walton be appointed for Cap Vances Company Thomas Harmand for Captain Pates Company, Peter Turney Esquire for Paytons Creek Company, Tilman Dixon Esquire for Captain Bradley Company, James Hibits Esquire for Captain Shaws Company & James Gwin Esquire for Captain Gwins Company.

Ordered that a tax of one dollar, be allowed each person for a Wolf Salp(Scalp) the Wolf being catch'd in Smith County they complying with the act of Assembly in that case made and provided.

Court then adjourned till tomorrow ten oclock.

Tuesday March the 18th Court met according adjournment. The following Gentlemen being present:Viz: Garret Fitsgerald,   Tilman Dixon
                      Charles Hudspeth &   Peter Turny's Esquire.

Ordered that Sampson Williams be allowed to record his Stock mark & brand, being a swallow fork in the left and his Brand the letters S. W.

Charles McClenen records his stock mark being a crop & slit in the right ear & an over keel in the left ear.

Deed Charles Mundine to Charles McClannen 92½ acres recorded And ordered to
p 8   be Registered, being proven by the oath of Jacob Bowerman one of the sub-scribing witnesses thereto.

Lease from Edmond Jinnings to Jacob Bowerman Ordered to be recorded.

Jacob Bowerman records his stock mark, being a crop of the left ear and a swallow fork in the right ear.

James Hibits records his stock mark, being a crop of the right ear a swallow fork and upper bit in the left ear.

Deed from George Wilson to Frederick Erick, was proven by the oath of Basel Shaw and ordered to be recorded.

Harden Gregory Stock mark a crop & slit in the left ear and a hole and half moon in the right ear, Ordered to be recorded.

Ordered that Henry Dancer be allowed to retail Spiritous Liquors at his own house on the same terms as other Tavern Keepers are rated in this County, which rates are to be in fource until next Court & no longer.

William Gregorys Stock mark a crop off the left ear Ordered to be recorded.

William Boyds Stock mark a swallowfork in each ear Ordered to be recorded.

James Dobbins stock mark a crop off the right ear and a half moon under the left ear ordered to be recorded.

David Mitchels Stock mark a crop off the left & a half moon under the left ear ordered to be recorded.

Ordered that the Grand Jury be Dismissed.

The Court appoints the following Gentlemen as a Venire to the ensuing County Court:viz: David Keilough, Richard Brittain Stephen Box, Danl. Alexander Blacksmith, Basel Shaw, John Murphy, William Stalcup, David Cochran, Robt. Bowman, Godfrey Fowler, Terrisha Turner, Elias Johns, Isom Beasley, Philip Day William Saunders, Vincient Ridley, Patrick Donoho, Robert (torn out), John Douglass, William Gregory,
p 9   Leonard Jones, Henry Duncan, Charles McClanan, Richard Harmon, James Cherry, Christopher Bullar, Stephen Pate, John Paterson, Goose Creek, John Rutherford, James Roberts, Edward Pate, Pleasant Kearby, Joel Dyer, Junr., Edmond Jinnings and Jacob Bowerman.

Ordered that Sampson Williams be appointed Guardian to Sarah Young who gave Security accordingly.

Ordered that Rachel Clark be appointed Guardian to her daughter, Dorcas, who gave bond & Security accordingly.

Zedekiah Ingram appointed Constable who gave bond & Security and quallified according to law.

Ordered that Charles McClenan be appointed Overseer of the Road where Jacob

Bowerman was Overseer, and that the same hands work under him as worked under Jacob Bowerman.

Ordered that Abraham Britten be appointed Overseer of a Road leading from Harts ferry to where it intersects the Road called the Kentucky Road to commence at the County line, and from thence to where it intersects the said Kentucky Road, and that all the hands West of Richard Brittins to the County line, down to the new road and all below the said Brittins on the west side of the middle fork of Goose Creek to the mouth thereof and down the main fork to said new Road.

Court adjourned until tomorrow morning nine oclock.

1800

Wednesday March the 19th Court met according to adjournment the following Gentlemen being present: viz: James Gwin,
        Talman Dixon,&
        Charles Hudspeth Esquires.

Ordered that Benjamin Blackburn be allowed to keep an ordinary at his now dwelling house and that he be rated as follows (viz) for good whisky or Brandy of proof quality 18¼ cents pr. half pint For Breakfast, Dinner, & Supper, 25 cents, For corn or oat pr. gallon 16¼ cents for Lodging Pr. each person pr. the P 10   night 8 1/3 cents, for fodder pr. 2 Bundles 6¼ cents. for Pasturage 24 hours 12½ cents.

Ordered that John Jenkins be allowed to keep an ordinary at his now dwelling house and that he be rated as all other retailors in said County except Mr. Blackburn, who gave bond & security accordingly.

Ordered that William Martin be appointed Guardian to John Young Son of William Young Deceased.

Ordered that William Martin, William Walton, John Bravard & Sampson Williams be appointed Guardian for Annie Young, James Young, Nancy Young, and Dice Young four of the Orphans of William Young Deceasd. all of whom came into Court and gave bond and security according to law,

Garret Fitzgerald records his Stock mark & Brand mark an under bit out of the left ear & over bit out of the same Brand P. F.

Deed Thomas Murry to James Hibits Ordered to be registered.

Recognizance of James Ballow taken before James Hibits, and Thomas Harmand on a charge against him by Polley Reynolds for Bastardy returned into Court and ordered to be filed of record.

Ordered that a road be layed off from Flyns Lick to the nearest settlement on Obeds River agreeable to law & that James Blackburn, James Jones, James Armistron William Dale, Enoch Fox, Sampson Williams, Moses Fisk, be appointed, as a Jury to view, mark, and lay off said road.

Ordered that a road be layed off agreeable to law from the Fort Blount road near the crossing of Salt Lick Creek to the nothern boundary of this State, near P 11   the head of the Salt Lick Fork of Barren River, and that Thomas Draper, James Draper, Jacob Bowerman, Jacob Jenkins, Pleasant Kearby, William Pate, Henry Huddleston and Sampson Williams be appointed as a Jury to view, mark and lay off said Road.

Ordered that a road be layed off from the Nothern boundary of this State, near Mr. Irons on Obeds River to intersect the road leading from Stocktons Valley, to Mr. Blackburns at the most convenient place, and that John Sprowls, William Dale,

Edward Irons, John Irons, and John Dale are appointed as a jury to lay off said road, and report the same to our ensuing court

Ordered that Henry McKinny, Garret Fitsgerald, Sampson Williams, James Blackburn, Uriah Anderson, James Jones, Thomas Jones, Edmund Jennings and Benjamin Blackburn be appointed to view mark & lay off a road from Fort Blount to Mr. Blackburns agreeable to law.

Ordered that William Walton, John Crosswhite, William Shaw, James Payne & John Campbell, are appointed to view mark and lay off a road from the mouth of Caney Fork, to the Indian boundary agreeable to law.

Ordered that William Martin, Grant Allen, and John Bravard be appointed as commissioners to settle with the County Trustee or such settlement when made to report to our said Court.

Ordered that David Venters be allowed to build a public mill on Goose Creek near the head of the big Spring which is between the forks of Goose Creek he complying with the law in that case made and provided.

Ordered that Anthony Pate be appointed overseer of the Road from Fort Blount
P 12   to Salt Lick Creek and that all the hands living below the crossing of said Creek between the said Road and the River & Creek and River are to work on said road.

Ordered that Moses Ashbrooks be appointed Overseer of the Road from the crossing of Salt Lick Creek, to the top of the ridge between s'd Creek and defeated Creek and all the hands that worked under Mr. Kearby are to work under said Overseer.

Ordered that Charles Mundines Stock mark be recorded :viz: both ears cropt and an under bit in the left ear.

Court then adjourned until Court in Course
Test   Garret Fitsgerald
Sampson Williams   Peter Turney
                                            James Hibits
                                            James Gwinn

Dixon Springs, Monday June the 16th 1800 - Court met according to adjournment
The following members being present: Viz: Garret Fitsgerald
                                            William Walton,
                                            Tilman Dixon and
                                            Charles Hudspeth Esquires.

Grand Jury Elected and sworn; Viz: John Douglass, foreman, Godfrey Fowler, Patrick Donoho, James Roberts, Robert Bowerman, John Paterson, Philip day, Jacob Bowerman, Richard Harmand, James Cherry, David Cochran, Leonard Jones, Stephen Pate, Edmund Jenning, Isham Beasley.

Ordered that Lemuel Henry, be admitted as a practising attorney he having taken the necessary Oaths & the oath of office.

Ordered that Silas Jernigan, be appointed as Constable to attend on the Grand Jury, who was accordingly sworn.

Deed 100 acres Thomas Harney to Escom Graves proven by the Oath of Jacob Bowerman one of the subscribing witness's thereto ordered to be registered.
P 13   Ordered that Thomas Draper Pleasant Kirby and Willeroy Pate, be appointed as patrollers for Captain Pates Company.

Ordered that Richard Banks be allowed to keep a ferry at his own landing below the mouth of Dixons Creek and that he be rated agreeable to the rates of all other ferries in thes County Except Edmond Jennings.

Will of Jesse Sanderson, proven by the oath of Arthur Hessian one of the Subscribers witness's thereto who also swore that he saw John Patterson subscribe the same as a witness with himself.

John Sanderson & Leonard Jones, sworn as Executors.

Ordered that Benjamin be appointed Constable who came into Court and gave security according to law and took the necessary oath.

William Marchbanks stock mark, both ears crossed and a slit in the right ordered to be recorded.

Ordered that a Jury be appointed to view, mark and lay off a road from where Russells Path crosses river, near the mouth to the nearest settlement on Obeds River, and that Charles Hedspeth John Overturf, Samuel Doneley & Sampson Williams view the same and make report thereof to our ensuing Court.

Ordered that Joel Dyer be allowed to Build a mill on Payton Creek on his own land.

Court then adjourned till tomorrow morning ten o'clock

Tuesday June 17th 1800 Court met according to adjournment The following Gentlemen being present (Viz) Garret Fitsgerald
                              Tilman Dixon
                              James Hibits,
                              Charles Hudspeth &
                              Peter Turney Esqr.

Ordered William Martin, George Strother & Robert Looney be appointed as inspectors to the Election for field Officers.

Ordered that James Dobbins be allowed a permit to retail Spiritous Liquors
P 14 until next Court, also that he be forever hereafter exempted from paying a poll Tax for himself.

Deed 450 acres, John Sevier & George Gordon to John McDaniel acknowledged by Gordon and proven by the oath of Nathaniel Evins as to Sevier Ordered to be Registered.

Deed 200 acres John Sevier & George Gordon to George Smith Acknowledged by Gordon & proven by the oath of John McDaniel as to Seviere Ordered to be Registered.

Ordered that all Strays brought to Court, be put into a Stray pen to be be shewn them by Major Dixon and there be kept agreeable to Law.

Major Tilman Dixon Stock mark a slit in each ear Ordered to be recorded.

Deed Francis Cypert Senr. to Francis Cypert Junr. proven by the oath of William Allen one of the Subscribing witness's thereto ordered to be Registered.

Letter of attorney Thomas Harris to Charles Harris, proven by the oath of Ephraim Davidson one of the subscribing witnesses thereto and ordered to be registered

P 15   Ordered that Grant Allen, Basil Shaw William Walton and William Saunders, be appointed commissioners, to take the Testimony of Uriah Anderson, Charles Carter & John Rains, to establish the claim of Elmore Douglas to a tract of Land on Dixons Creek, beginning at William's Camp runs up the east fork for Compliment.

Deed 228 acres Sampson Williams to George Thomason acknowleged Ordered to be registered.

Deed Redmond D. Barry to Sampson Williams for 228 acres proven by the oath of Michael Murphy one of the subscribing witnesses thereto and ordered to be registered.

Benjamin Totten(?) took the oath of Deputy Sheriff in Open Court.

Ordered that Jonas Dancer be allowed a permit to retail Spirituous until next Court and no longer, and that he be rated agreeable to the common rates in this County.

Court adjourned until Tomorrow ten o'clock.

Wednesday June the 18th 1800 - Court met according to adjournment. The following members being present: viz: Garret Fitsgerald
James Gwin,
Charles Hudspeth,
James Hibits and
Peter Turney Esquire

Ordered that William Keltons Stock mark & Brand a half crop in the under side of the left ear and an over and an under Slope in the left ear. Brands for Cattle (K) & for horses thus (W.K.) Ordered to be recorded.

Ordered that the report of a Jury to view & lay off a road from the mouth of the Cansy fork to the Indian Boundary be received and filed on record.

A Venire to the ensuing Court appointed (to wit) David Keilow, Henry King, P 16 William Gregory, John Gray, David White, John Chambers, Benjamin Johns, William Simpson, Jeremiah Taylor, Reuben Alexander, Edward Settles, Michael Murphy, Arthur Hessian, Josiah Payne, Philip Day, Charles Thompson, John Johnson, Charles McMurry, Joel Dyer, Christopher Bullar, John Steel, James Vance, Uriah Anderson, Lee Sullivan, William Staloup, Archibald Donoho, Frances Finley, George Thompson, Frederick Turner, Hugh Stephenson, John Campbell, John Fisher, Thomas Walker, Francis Patterson, James Gibson and Thomas Draper.

Report of a Jury to lay off a road from Dixons Spring to the mouth of White Oak, on the State line by James Gwin Ordered to be received to be received and filed of record.

Ordered that Samuel Corrothers be appointed Overseer of the road from Mungles gap to the ridge at the head of a branch of the East fork of Goose Creek. Also that Robert Looney be appointed Overseer from thence to the Maple Slashes, near John Fisher. Also that Levi Cass be appointed Overseer, from thence to the State line. Also ordered that James Gwin & James Hibits Esquires, be appointed to furnish said Overseers, with a list of the polls to work under said Overseers.

Ordered that Terisha Turner be appointed Overseer of the road from the Ridge, between Defeated & Payton's Creek to Michael Murphy's. Also that Christian Boston, be appointed Overseer from Michael Murphy's to the Ridge, between Paytons & Dixons Creek and that Peter Turney Esquire, be appointed to furnish said Overseers with a list of polls to work under said Overseers.

Daniel Mingles Stock mark a smooth crop of the left ear ordered to be recorded.

P 17   Ordered that the Court Adjourn <u>untill</u> Court in Course to meet at Michael Murphys on Paytons Creek.
Teste   Garret Fitsgerald
Sampson Williams   Thomas Harmand
                                             Charles Hudspeth
                                             James Hibits

    Paytons Creek, Monday September 15th 1800 Court met according to adjournment, the following members being present: viz: Garret Fitsgerald,
                                             Tilman Dixon,
                                             Moses Fisk,
                                             James Hibits,
                                             Thomas Harman, &
                                             Peter Turney Esquires.

    John Chambers foreman of the Grand Jury, John Fisher, Francis Paterson, Frederick Turner, William Gregory, David Keilough, Charles McMurry, Arthur Hessian, Hugh Stephenson, William Simpson, Francis Findley, Jeremiah Taylor, Joes Dyer, Edward Settles, Grand Jury Elected and sworn.

    And Silas Jernigan, Constable sworn to attend them.

    Ordered that Michael Murphy be allowed a licence to keep an ordinary at his now dwelling house, and <u>the</u> be rated agreeable to the common rates within this County.

    Bond Martin Armstrong to Josiah Payne ordered to be recorded.

    Ordered that Nicholas Perkins be admitted as a practitioner of the Law, he having produced a licence in due form.

    Deed 400 acres John Matheral, to Lee Sullivan, was proven by the oath of Willie Sullivan, one of the subscribing witnesses thereto let it be registered.

    Letter of Attorney Josiah <u>Ridditt</u> to Thomas Howell Ordered to be recorded.

P. 18   Ordered that Robert Price be appointed Constable, who came into Court gave security & <u>qualifyed</u> according to law.

    Robert Prices stock mark, two smooth crops & two slits in each ear ordered to be recorded.

    Ordered that Tilman Dixon, Henry McKinney, Peter Turney, and William Saunders be appointed as a Venire faceas to the Superior Court.

    Ordered that John B. Johnson be allowed as a practitioner of the law, he having produced a Licence authenticated in manner prescribed by law.

    Ordered that Thomas Armistrong Vincent Ridley & Godfrey Fowler be appointed as Searchers, or Overseers of the Patrolls in Captain Bradleys Company.

    Court then adjourned tomorrow nine o'clock
                                             Sampson Williams Clk.

    Tuesday September the 16th 1800 Court met according to adjournment the following members being present (towit) Garrett Fitsgerald, Moses Fisk and
                                             Moses Fisk and
                                             James Hibits Esquires.

The court then proceeded to business, and ordered that James Gwin, James Hibits and Major Andrew Greer, be appointed commissioners to take the deposition of the said James Gwin, Sampson Williams and Joel Echols, to establish the claim of Josiah Howell to 688 acres of land on the Ridge between the head of Goose Creek & Barron River.

Ordered that James Ballow be appointed Overseer of the road from the top of the ridge, between Paytons & Dixons Creek, to the fords of Dixons Creek near his own house by way of the new road and that all Colo Martins hands Capt. Turneys & his own work under said Overseer and that all the ballance of the hands living above said new road on the waters of Dixons Creek, to work under John Hargiss who is appointed Overseer from said ford of Dixons Creek, near Cap. Ballows to the top of the ridge in Mingles Gap &c.

P 19

Ordered that Edward Settles, record his Stock mark: viz: a swallow fork in the right ear & a crop & slit in the left ear.

Ordered that Arthur Hessian's Stock mark be recorded (towit) two half crops in both ears.

Ordered that Peter Turney Esquires Stock mark be recorded: viz: a swallow fork in the left ear and an under half crop and a small upper bit in the right.

Deed for 125 acres George Gordon & John Sevier to Phileman Higgins Acknowledged by Gordon & Strother as attorneys for Seviers ordered to be registered.

Ordered William Saunders be allownaced to build a Saw & Grist Mill on Dixons Creek, about 200 yards below the blue Spring under the following restrictions (to wit) the Dam not to be more than twelve feet high, the water to be drawn off as requested by Maj. Dixon by the fifteenth of June in each year.

Court adjourned until tomorrow ten o'clock Paytons Creek Wednesday September the 17th 1800 - Court met according to adjournment. the following Members being present: viz: Tilman Dixon,
Moses Fisk
Peter Turney
James Hibbits Esquires

Court then proceeded to business, And ordered that James Draper be appointed Overseer of the road lately Layed off from Salt Lick Creek to the Kentucky line, as far as to tandy Witchers also that James Simpson als that James Simpson is appointed overseer of Said road From Witchers to the said line, and that all the hands living on Salt Lick, Defeated & Wartract Creek, to work under Draper, & that all the hands living on Jennings Creek, as low down as William Keltons and George Thomasons including them & their hands, to work under said overseer also those on the ridge convenient to said road.

P 20

Ordered that Amos Lacey be allowed to resign his appointment as Constable.

Bill of Sail Anne Smith to Sampson Williams was proven by the Oath of Garret Fitzgerald, the Subscribing witnesses thereto, ordered to be recorded.

Ordered that Jonas Dancer be allowed a permit to retail Spirituous at the costomary rates within this County until next Court.

Ordered that James Dobbins, John Steel William Stalcup & Uriah Anderson be allowed a permit to retail Spirituous Liquors within this County at the customary rates of Tavern Keepers within said County until next Court.

Ordered that Robert Hill be appointed Overseer of the road from the Nothern boundary of this State to the head of Mitchels Creek and that all the hands work under said Overseer adjoining thereto to out out and work on the same and that John Bowen be appointed Overseer from the head of Mitchels Creek to Captains Copelands and that the hands adjacent thereto, open and work on the same under said Overseer.

Ordered that William Sullivan Senr. be appointed Overseer of the road from Sullivans ferry to the forks of said road to where it meets Waltons Road and that all the hands living on Martin Indian and Hurricane Creek work under said Overseer on said road.

P 21   Ordered that John McDaniel, Nathaniel Evins, John Morgan, Stephen Copeland, and Simon Huddleston be appointed view mark and lay off a road from Mr. Blackburns to Robert Eliotts on the nothern Boundary of the State, where the road cut by Cap Gordon intersects it.

Ordered that Christian Bostons Stock mark be recorded which is a Swallow fork in the left ear & a Slit in the right.

George Thomason Stock mark a Swallowfork in the right ear and a crop & under keel in the left ear. Ordered to be recorded.

Ordered that Court adjourn hereafter for the four next Succeeding Courts alternately first to Fort Blount and next to Dixons Springs.

Venire faceas to the next ensuing Court ; viz: Christopher Bullar John Fitzgerald, Henry McKinny, William Anderson, Uriah Anderson, Charles Carter, William Marchbanks, Joseph Williams, Michael Williamson, Samuel McCollester, Jabias Fitzgerald, Willeroy Pate, James Roberts, Thomas Heaton, Jacob Jenkins Esom Graves Pleasant Kearby, Edward Pate, Booker Pate Jas & Daniel Draper John Jenkins, William Richards, Charles McClellen, Charles Mundine, Philip Draper, Thomas Jenkins Lee Sullivan William Ashbrooks, James Rooland, Henry Wakefield, Jacob Bowerman, James Blackburn, John Williams, Charles Oniel and John Anderson.

John McDonnald produced a commission from his Excellency the Governor appointing the said McDonald as a Justice of the Peace in and for the County of Smith, bearing date the 29th day of August 1800 and offered to quallify But the Court abjected against his quallifying on the ground of his appointment being unconstitutional.

Deed for 640 acres Sampson Williams to Charles Hudspeth Acknowleged Ordered to be registered.

P 22   Ordered that the resignation of Tandy Wicher as Constable be received.

Court adjourns until Court in counse to meet at fort Blount on the third Monday in December next.
    Test   T. Dixon
    Sampson Williams   W. Walton
                                        P. Turney.

Fort Blount Monday December the 15th 1800 Court met according to adjournment the following Members being present (Towit) Garret Fitsgerald
                                        Charles Hudspeth,
                                        Thomas Hammand, and
                                        Peter Turney Esquire.

The Court then proceeded to business and the Venire being called the following Gentlemen were Elected as Grand Jurors, :viz: James Roberts, John Jinkins, Charles McClennen Pleasant Kearby William Marchbanks, Edward Pate, William Anderson, Charles

Carter, Christopher Bullar, Stephen Pate Esom Graves Jacob Jinkins, Willeroy Pate, John Fitsgerald and John Anderson and James Roberts being appointed foreman of the Said Grand Jury Henry Huddleston was appointed to attend them.

Ordered that Court adjourn until tomorrow nine oclock.

Tuesday December the 16th 1800 Court met according to Adjournment the following Members being present: Viz: Charles Hudspeth,
Thomas Harmand,
James Hibits.

On motion of Peter Turney by his Attorney Ordered that the Sheriff be directed to Summon a Jury on the premises of a disputed tract of Land Claimed by the Said Peter Turney and Willie Cherry Caveators & And Armistead Stubblefield Cavitee, agreeable to a Certificate of William White Secretary of the State of North Carolina in the words follwwing (towit) State of North Carolina William White Secretary of the State To the worshipful the Justices of Smith County Greeting - whereas his Excellency the Governor hath certified to me that on the complaints of Peter Turney & Armistead Stubblefield on oath he has suspended the execution of a Grant to Willie Cherry for six hundred and forty acres of Land in your said County on the East Side of a small creek called Spring Creek running East & North for compliment So as to include Boyds improvement Military Warrent No 3116 Entered 19th of May 1800 and directed me to certify the suspension of the Execution of the Grant to you the said Justices to the end the controversy be determined according to law.

I therefore hereby certify the Execution of Said Grants to the Said Willie Cherry for the Said Land accordingly Given under my hand at Raligh the 18th Sept 1800.
Will White Secy.

Ordered that Samuel Huff Senr. be allowed Letters of Administration to administer on the Estate of John Lee who gave bond and Security & quallified according to law.

Ordered that Henry McKinney, James Dobbins, William Stalcup Senr. John Steel, Michael Osburn & Uriah Anderson be allowed permits Severally to retail Spirituous Liquors at each of their dwelling Houses until next Court They complying with the Court rates.

Silas Jernigan took the oath of Deputy Sheriff, and also the oath to support the Constitution of the United States & the State of Tennessee.

Ordered that John Reid be appointed Overseer of the road leading from Mingles gap to the Summer line, and that Peter Turney be appointed to furnish a list of hands &c.

Ordered that John Steel be appointed Overseer of the road from Fort Blount to the top of the ridge at the head of Flins Creek and that all the hands subject to work under the late Overseer of said road to work under said Overseer.

Ordered that Samuel Corrothers be appointed Overseer of the road from Mingles Gap to the ford of the East fork of Goose Creek and that David Keilough be appointed Overseer of the same from Said ford to the far side of the first can break on the Ridge. And Aaron Hart be appointed Overseer of the road from the last mentioned place to the Maple Slashes opposite John Fisher, And that Andrew Greer be appointed Overseer of the left hand fork of said road from Richard Brittains & that James Hibits Esquire furnish said Overseers with a list of hands.

Court Adjourns until tomorrow nine oclock.

Wednesday the 17th Court met according to adjournment The following Gentlemen being present: viz: Garret Fitsgerald,
James Hibits,
Peter Turney Esquires

Ordered that James Jones who was bound to this Term on the Complaint of Phoeby Snodgrass for begetting a child on her body be rebound for the maintainance of the said child and that he be bound to pay the said Phebee Snodgrass the sum of twenty five dollars to defray the Expenses of her lying (inn) and maintaining her child until it is one year old. And sixteen & tw third dollars annually until the child is three years old. And that he give sufficient security for his complying with the above order. When Uriah Anderson & William Robertson, came into Court and Acknowleged themselves his securities for complying with the above order.

Bond Sampson Williams to Anne Smith Acknowledged in open Court & Ordered to be recorded.

Ordered that Thomas Harmand Charles Mundine Charles McClennen, Willcroy Pate, P 25   Robert Rowland, Charles Dillard, John Williamson & William Sullivan Junr. be appointed a Jury to view, mark & lay off a road from the Fort Blount road to Waltons Road by way of Sullivans ferry & report the same to our ensuing Court.

Charles Carters Stock mark, a crop off the right ear and under bit in the lift. Ordered to be recorded.

Deed 250 acres William Sullivan to John Williamson proven by the oath of Joseph Williamson one of the subscribing witnesses thereto.

Deed 1400 Acres Samuel Parker to Garrett Fitsgerald Proven by the oath of John L. Martin.

Deed Garret Fitsgerald to Christopher 400 Acres Acknowleged.

Deed 200 Acres Christopher Bullar to William Roberts and Acknowledged & ordered to be registered.

Ordered that Henry McKenny, Sampson Williams, James Blackburn Benjamin Blackburn Uriah Anderson John Fitsgerald, Tabias Fitsgerald & Barnett Lee be appointed to view, mark & lay off a road from Fort Blount to the Indian Boundary near Mr. Blackburns and that they report the same to our ensuing County Court.

Ordered that Moses Fisk & Sampson Williams be appointed to survey a disputed claim of Land between John Seviere & George Gordon Plaintiff and Alexander Suit Defendant and they or either of them to act Seperately or jointly.

Ordered that Smith Huchings be appointed of the road from the top of the ridge at the head of Flins Creek, to the Indian Boundary near Mr. Blackburns & that Garret Fitsgerald Esquire furnish a list of hands.

P 26 On motion of Alexander McCulloch one of the Heirs of Benjamin McCulloch Deceased grounded on the affidvit of the Said Alexander M.Culloch it is ordered that the Heirs of the said Benjamin M Culloch shall now be at liberty to deliver in to the Clerk of this Court, a list of taxable property belonging to the heirs of the said Benjamin for the present year. And that the List so given in shall be considered by relation, as having been given in at September Term of this Court, and that said list with the Clerk, & immediately paying the tax of the same into the hands of the Clerk be thereupon discharged from the fine & double Tax.

Ordered that Sampson Williams, William Anderson Thomas Heaton, Charles Carter

William Marchbanks & James Carter be appointed to view mark & lay off a road from where T. William Anderson lives to Mr. Pates Horse Mill & report the same to our ensuing Court

Ordered that John Overturf, John Black, Samuel Huff Abr. Denton & Stephen Copeland be appointed a Jurty to view mark & lay off a road from where the Kentucky road intersects line creek the nearest & best way to Captains Stephen Copelands on Roaring River and report the same to our ensuing Court.

The following Gentlemen were appointed as a Venire to our ensuing Court -: Viz: William Martin, Grant Alen James Ballow, Daniel Hammonck, William Saunders, John Patterson Patrick Donoho, Thomas Walker, William Roper, William Kelton, John Gray, Thomas Bowerman, Godfrey Fowler, William Hayney, John Chambers, William Stalcup, John Stafford, James Bradley, Andrew Greer, Richard Brittain, Jeremiah Taylor, Philip Day, Charles McMurry, Anthony Samuel, John Murphy, John Brevard P 27 David Keilough Jun., Daniel Mungle, John Johnson, James Gibson, John Reid Samuel Corothers, John Rutherford, Robert Bowman Abraham Brittain John Doughlass.

Court Adjourns until <u>until</u> the third Monday in March to meet at Dixon Springs.
Sampson Williams Clk.

Dixons Springs Monday March 16th 1801 Court met according to adjournment, present Garret Fitsgerald,
  Tilman Dixon,
  Moses Fisk,
  James Hibits,
  Peter Turney Esquire

Ordered that, Michael Osburn be allowed an ordinary License at his own house & that he be rated as above, who gave bond and security according to law.

Deed 250 acres William Saunders to Benjamin Gist Acknowleged and ordered to be registered.

Deed 186 acres John Caffrey & George M. Deadrick to Francis Weatheread(?) proven by the oath of James Espey one of the subscribing witnesses thereto, and ordered to be registered.

Deed 186 Francis Witherhead to Josiah Wood - Acknowleged and ordered to be registered.

Two Deeds 640 acres each Benjamin Dren(?) to Stephen Montgomery and James McKain, proven by the oath of Jacob Grass one of the subscribing witnesses thereto and ordered to be registered.

Deed 250 acres George M. Deadrick & John Caffary to Samuel Coruthers, proven by the oath of Jesse Wharton one of the subscribing witnesses thereto & ordered to be registered.

Deed 289 acres John Dawson to, Thomas Johnson proven by the the oath of Alen Wilkinson one of the subscribing witnesses thereto and ordered to be registered.

P 28   The following Gentlemen was drawn as Grand Jurors: viz: Andrew Greer foreman William Haney, William Ropher, Richard Brittain, John Gray Robert Bowman, Abraham Brittain, Patrick Donoho, Grant Allen, Philip Day, Daniel Mungle, William Stalcup, Samuel Coruthers, Anthony Samuel and John Stafford - Robert Cotton Constable sworn to attend on the Grand Jury.

Deed 450 acres Robert Hays to John Murphy proven by the oath of David White one of the subscribing witnesses thereto and ordered to be registered.

Deed 100 acres James Ballow to John Gray proven by the oath of David Rorax(?) one of the subscribing witnesses thereto & ordered to be registered.

Deed 240 acres James Ballow to Edmond Boze proven by the oath of David Rorax(?) one of the subscribing witnesses thereto ordered to be registered.

Deed 140 Acres Edmond Boze to David Roarax(?) Acknowleged and ordered to be regestered.

Ordered that the Court inter into the following rule (towit) that in all suits in future, the parties shall be ruled to try or continue all causes on which Issue is joined the first day of the said cause comes on in term.

Deed 330 Acres John Seviere & George Gordon to Edward Crofford proven by the oath of the subscribing witness thereto Ordered to be registered.

Deed 200 John Seviers & Gordon to Harmon Cragg proven by the oath of the subscribing witnesses thereto & ordered to be registered.

Deed 66 8 Acres Elias Fort to Josiah Howell proven by the oath of Joel Holland one of the subscribing witnesses thereto ordered to be registered.

P 29   Deed Josiah Howell to Joel Holland 340 Acres Acknowledged and ordered to be registered.

Ordered that the following Justices be appointed to take a list of the taxable property for the present year (towit) James Hibits Esquire for the two lower Goose Creek Companies - Tilman Dixon for Cap Ballows Company, Peter Turney for Cap Settles & Cap Pates Companies, William Walton Esquire for Captian Priors Company Garret Fitsgerald Esquire for Cap Fitsgerald, Charles Hudspeth Esquire for the lower Obeds River Company & that Moses Fisk Esquire be appointed for Captain Russells Company & the upper Obeds River Company.

Ordered that there be a County tax of 6¼ cents laid on each 100 acres of Land 6¼ cents on each white poll, 12½ cents on each black poll and fifty cents on each Stud horse for the present year.

Ordered that Garrett Fitsgerald be allowed to build a mill on Flins Creek upon his own Land.

Deed John Seviere & George Gordon to Benjamin Tatten(?) 280 acres proven by the oath of John McDonald one of the subscribing witnesses thereto & ordered to be registered.

Ordered that Court adjourn until tomorrow nine oclock.

Tuesday March the 17th Court met according to adjournment Members present (towit) William Walton,
                  Moses Fisk and
                  Peter Turney Esqr.

On motion of George Smith Esq. ordered that the fine & Double tax incurred by George M. Deadrick on 500 acres of Land be remitted for the year Eighteen hundred.

John Ratcliff Security for Paul Garrison surrendered him in open court & the
P 30   Court ordered him into the custody of the Sheriff.

On motion of Benjamin Seawell Esquire ordered that the fine & double tax incurred by John Sedsley for John Williams on 800 acres of Land for the year 1800 be remitted.

Deed 100 Acres Abram Thompson to John Hargiss proven by the oath of John Reid one of the subscribing witnesses thereto and ordered to be registered.

Deed 2 acres Thomas Walker & Griffith Rutherford to David Venters, proven by the oath of Francis Look one of the subscribing witnesses thereto and ordered to be registered.

Deed 100 acres George M. Deadrick and John Caffery to Frances Patterson proven by the oath of James Gibson one of the subscribing witnesses thereto & ordered to be registered.

Deed John Caffery & George M. Deadrick to William Moore 50 acres proven by the oath of Francis Patterson one of the subscribing witnesses and ordered to be registered.

Deed George M. Deadrick & John Caffery to James Gibson 100 acres proven by the oath of Francis Patterson one of the subscribing witnesses thereto & ordered to be registered.

Deed 50 Acres Henry W. Lawson to Barnibas Powell proven by the Oath of John Vines one of the subscribing witnesses thereto & ordered to be registered.

Ordered that that William Staloup be appointed Overseer of the same part of the road where John Shelton was Overseer & and the same hands work under said Staloup as was liable to work under said Shelton.

Charles F. Mabias Stock mark and Brand, the mark a crop off the left ear and half crop in the right & the hand thus C.M. ordered to be recorded.

Benjamin Tatten, delivered up Wm. Livingston for whom Appearance Bail – P 31 Deed 200 Acres William Walton to Augustine Carter Acknowleged & ordered to be registered.

Ordered that Martha Scuff (Acuff) be appointed Guardian to her Daughter Sarah, & that Jabas (Jabias) Gifford be appointed Guardian to John Acuff Son to Martha Acuff both of whom gave security according to Law.

Deed 100 Acres William Saunders to John Johnson acknowleged and ordered to be registered.

Deed John Reed to Wm. Saunders for 100 Acres proven by the oath of Francis Look one of the subscribing witnesses thereto And ordered to be registered.

Ordered that the Grand Jury be discharged from farther attendance.

Court Adjourns until tomorrow nine oclook.

Wednesday March the 14th 1801 Court met according to Adjournment Members present: viz: William Walton
          Tilman Dixon,
          Moses Fisk,
          James Hibits and
          Peter Turney Esquires.

Ordered that John Martin Esquire be allowed $80 for his Exofficio services as Sheriff for the year 1800.

Ordered that Joseph Russell be appointed Constable who gave security &
qualified according to law.

Ordered that Anthony Samuel be appointed Overseer of the road, where David
Cochran was overseer and that the same hands work under him as worked under the
late Overseer.

Ordered that William Gregory Joel Dyer Senr. James Simpson, Henry Webster,
John Patterson & William Jenkins be appointed as a Jury to view, mark & lay off
a Road from Paynes ferry at the mouth of Paytons Creek to Daniel Wichers by the
P 32 way of Michael Murphys, and that they report the same to our ensuing Court.

Ordered that Elisha Oglesby, Richard Brittain, Jeremiah Taylor, Andrew Greer,
Samuel Coruthers, Daniel Mingle, Owen Sullivan, and William Denny be appointed to
view mark & lay off a road agreeable to Law, from Samuel Coruthers, up the middle
fork of Goose Creek to the Ridge thence to long Creek, & to puncheon Camp and to
the Kentucky line.

On motion of John Hamilton & Jesse Wharton Esquires to tax the plaintiff
with all the costs of the suit Frederick Debo against James Vance on an appeal
from the Judgment of a Single Justice except the costs that accrued before said
Justice, and upon solemn argument the Court determined that the said Plaintiff
should pay all the cost that accrued on said appeal & Execution awarded accordingly.

Ordered that Peter Turny Esquire Daniel Mingle and John Brevard be appointed
Commissioners to settle with the administrators of Kain Acuff Dec. and that they
return such settlement to our ensuing County Court together with vouchers they
may receive.

Ordered that John Furlong be allowed $7\frac{1}{2}$ dollars for keeping a child left at
his house by a woman whose name is unknown or her place of abode the child being
about six weeks old, provided he furnish said child with a sufficient quantity
of cloathing and keep it comfortably for three months.

De-Po- for Plaintiff in the suit Wm. Kelton vs. Terrisha Turner to take
depositions of Robert Kelton in North Carolina thirty days notice.

Ordered that the Court Adjourn until tomorrow 9 oclock.

P 33 ·Tuesday March the 19th Court met according to adjournment Members present
William Walton,
Tilman Dixon,
Moses Fisk and
James Hibits Esquires.

On motion of George Smith & John C. Hamilton Esquires to grant a new trial
in the suit John L. Martin vs Michael Murphy and on solemn arguments heard as
well on the part of the Plaintiff as the Defendant. the Court decided that no
new trial be granted.

Ordered that Hugh Lamb[?] be appointed Overseer of the road lately laid out,
from Stephen Capelands to where the northern Boundary of the State crosses line
creek, to begin at said Copelands to the head of Mill creek And that John Overturf
be appointed Overseer from the head of Mill Creek to Cumberland River and that
Moses Fisk Esquire be appointed to furnish said Overseers with a list of hands.
And that John Black be appointed Overseer from Cumberland River to where the
nothern Boundary of the State crosses line creek & that all the hands living above

the waters of Jennings Creek on the North side of Cumberland River work under said Overseer.

Ordered that Harmon Grags be appointed overseer of the road lately laid off by John McDonald, Simon Huddleston, and John Morgan to begin on the south bank of Obeds River, to the top of the Ridge at the head of Eagle Creek and that all the hand living between Izons(Irons?) road and then Indian Boundary on the south side of Obeds River work under said Overseer. And that George Smith be appointed Overseer of the said road from the North bank of Obeds River to the State line and that the hands living within the following bounds. Beginning where the State line crosses Spring Creek thence a direct line to Obeds River to the Indian boundary and along the same to where it intersects the Nothern boundary of the State & north along the same to the Beginning.

P 34

In the Suit Jordan Roach against Lazarus Cotton on motion of the Deft Attorney for a new trial in the above suit, and on solemn argument had as well on behalf of the Plaintiff as the Defs. the Court decided that a new trial be granted.

Ordered that in the suit John L. Martin against Michael Murphy, all the costs which accrued in the above suit by summoning witnesses who have not attended together with the cost for issuing such Subpoenas be taxed on the Plaintiff.

Peter Turney & Armistead Stubblefield Caviators against Willis Cherry Caviatee on motion of the Deft. Attorney to set aside the Jury who attended upon the premises, and to order a new Jury to be summoned the Court overruled the motion and confirmed the verdict of said Jury.

In the suit John Seviere & George Gordon against Aron Robbins Benjamin Seawell Esquire moved to amend the Declaration in Ejectments. The Court determined that no amendments should be made and that the suit Abate accordingly by the agreement of the Plaintiffs Attorney.

Ordered that Moses Fisk Esquire and Sampson Williams Be appointed survey a disputed claim wherein George Gordon & John Seviere are plaintiffs and Alexander Suit Defendant and the said Surveyors meet on the 15th day of April next at the house of John Sprowls and that the Plffs. be directed to furnish said Surveyors with all the title papers to Establish their claim.

Ordered that the following Gentlemen be appointed on the Venire to the Superior Court: viz: Andrew Greer, Daniel Mingle David Cochran and Edward Settles.

A Venire for the ensuing County Court: viz: Thomas Draper, James Draper, Henry Huddleston, Lee Sullivan William Sullivan, William Anderson, Uriah Anderson, John Fitzgerald, Christopher Bullar William Robertson, Willeroy Pate Edward Pate, Booker Pate James Roberts, Isaac Green, Jacob Bowerman, Charles McClennen, William Marchbank, William Kelton, Elijah Hedgcock, John Steel, Nathaniel Ridley Thomas Keaton, Henry McKinney, Charles Carter, Thomas Williamson, Exom Graves, Jacob Jinkins, George Ashbrooks, James Fisher, James Armstrong, Thomas Wallace, Henry Sadler William Holiday, George Leeper, and Benjamin Holiday

P 35

Ordered that Moses Fisk, Grant Allen, and Peter Turney Esqr. be appointed Commissioners to settle with the Administrators of the Estate of William Young Deceas'd. that they report such settlement together with the vouchers relative thereto into our ensuing County Court

Pleasant Kearby & wife vs Philip Draper & wife on motion of the defendants Attorney the above Suit abated on the pleas of the Defendant.

Ordered that the fine & double tax incurred on 640 Acres of land lying on Roaring River be remitted for the year 1800.

Ordered that William Russell, James Taylor, Smith Hechings, John Bowen John M. Roberts John Burlison, Isham Russell & Stephen Capeland be Appointed a Jury to view, mark & lay off a road agreeable to law from or near the head of Eagle Creek where where the Road lately marked by John McDonald & others stops to intersect the Fort Blount Road at the most convenient place for the Roaring River Settlement And that they report the same to our ensuing County Court.

Ordered that Silas Jernigan Peter Turney, Tilman Dixon Nathaniel Dickerson and Moses Fisk, be appointed a Jury to view mark and lay off a road agreeable to law from Dixon Spring to Peter Turneys & that they report the same to our ensuing Court.

Ordered that Court adjourn to Fort Blount until Court in Course.
                                        Sampson Williams.

P 36   Fourt Blount Monday June the 15th 1801 Court met according to adjournment
Members present, James Hibits,
                 James Gwin &
                 Charles Hudspeth Esquires.

Ordered that Joseph Lock be allowed to keep a ferry at the mouth of Roaring on Cumberland River and that he be rated agreeable to rates of Smith County.

Ordered that Andrew Greer be allowed Letters of Administration to administer on the Estate of John Burke Dec'd who entered into bond & Security according to Law.

The following Gentlemen were Elected & sworn as a Grand Jury (towit) James Roberts foreman, Jacob Bowerman Henry McKinney, William Marchbanks, George Ashbrooks Thomas Draper William Holliday, Isaac Green, Edward Pate, Esom Graves, George Leeper, Charles McClennon Benjamin Holliday.

Ordered that Benjamin Price be appointed Constable to attend the Grand Jury who was sworn accordingly.

Deed 640 Acres Edward Leech to Elijah Evins proven by the oath of Thomas Summers one of the subscribing witnesses thereto And ordered to be registered.

Deed 157 acres John Williamson to John Sedgley proven by the oath of Willis Whitefield one of the subscribing witnesses thereto & ordered to be registered.

Deed 200 acres William Sullivan Senr. to William Sullivan Junr. proven by the Oath of James Sullivan Junr. proven by the Oath of James Sullivan one of the subscribing witnesses thereto & ordered to be registered.

William Hammond's Stock mark two swallowforks ordered to be recorded.

Deed 320 acres Richard & Thomas Harmond to William Holiday proven by the oath
P 37   of Willeroy Pate & Benjamin Holliday the subscribing witness thereto Ordered to be registered.

Willeroy Pates stock mark a crop & upper bit of each ear Ordered to be registered.

William Hollidays stock mark and under bit & slit in each ear Ordered to be registered.

Benjamin Seawell Esquire resigned his appointment as County Solicitor Ordered to be recorded Ordered that Jesse Wharton Esquire be appointed County Solicitor protempore for the County of Smith.

Court Adjourns until Tomorrow nine oclock.

Tuesday June the 16th 1801 - Court met according to adjournment Members present (viz) James Gwin
                    Charles Hudspeth
                    James Hibbits,
                    Peter Turney, Esquire.

Ordered that the Inventory of John Lee Dec'd. returned by Saml. Huff Administrator be received & entered of record.

Ordered that Sampson Williams, be appointed to survey a Tract of Land claimed by George Gordon & John Seviere whereon Alexander Suit now lives, and that he return three Just & fair plans thereof into our ensuing Court.

Deed 325 acres Samuel Parker to John Fitsgerald proven by the oath of John L. Martin one of the subscribing witnesses thereto Ordered to be registered.

Deed 122 Acres Edmond Jinnings to Daniel Draper proven by the oath of James Roberts one of the subscribing witnesses thereto and Ordered to be registered.

Ordered that James Crabtree be appointed Overseer of the Road lately layed off from Daniel Wichers to the state Line near to the State line near Gisses settlement to begin at said Wichers and that all the hands on the waters of Jinnings Creek work under said Overseer.

P 38   Deed 750 Acres Selby Harney to Timothy Ridley proven by the oath of Armistead Stubblefield one of the subscribing witnesses thereto Ordered to be Registered.

Ordered that William Martin be appointed Overseer of the Road from the top of the Ridge between Martins & Dixons Creek to the ford of Dixons Creek near Cap Ballows and that the following hands work under said Overseer (viz) all his own Captain Turney Cap Ballows, Vincient Ridley Thomas Sutton Leonard Ballow, Jacob Hancock, Godfrey Fowler David Rorax & John Gray work under said Overseer.

Ordered that John McCormack be appointed Overseer of half the Road lately laid off From Daniel Witchers to the State line near Guesses settlement And that all the hands on Bowen adjacent to the Road work under Said Overseer.

Bill of Sail James Lee to Sampson Williams was proven by the oath of John L. Martin one of the subscribing witnesses thereto and ordered to be recorded.

Ordered that Robert Bowman be appointed Overseer of the Road from the ford of Paytons Creek where Waltons Road crosses the same to Saunders ferry & that all the hands that worked under William Saunders that lives between Dry Creek & Payton Creek work under said Overseer.

Ordered that Big Joel Dyer be appointed Overseer of the Road from Michael Murphy's to the mouth of Paytons Creek and that William Walton Esq. furnish said Overseer with a list of hands.

Bill of Sail Joseph Teas to Henry McKinney proven by the oath of Jas. Blackburn & ordered to be recorded.

Ordered that Benjamin Blackburn be allowed to keep an ordinary at his now
P 39 dwelling house at the Double Springs and that he be rated agreeable at his

last year rates, who gave bond and security.

Bond Williams Dec'd to Hardy Williams proven by the oath of Peter Turney one of the subscribing witnesses.

Ordered that a Road from William Andersons on Martins Creek be laid out agreeable to law & that the following Jury view the same William Anderson, William Marchbanks, Thomas Keaton, Sampson Williams, Charles Carter, and James Carter, and that they report the same to our ensuing Court.

Ordered that the Grand Jury be discharged from further attendance.

Deed 400 acres Michael Murphy & wife & William Marchbanks to Hardy Williams Acknowleged in Court and ordered that the same be certified to the County Court of Lee in Virginia.

Ordered that the following hands be liable to work under John Steel Overseer of the Road from Fort Blount to the top of the Ridge at the head of Flins Creek (towit) Christopher Bullar & William Robertsons hands and all as high up the River so as to include Chaffins Settlement and all the hands on the waters of Flinns Creek.

Barnet Lees Stock Mark an underkeel in the right and also a swallowford. an overkeel in the left ear ordered to be recorded.

Allen Watkinsons Stock mark crop off the left ear and a hole in the right and Brand Letter (W) Ordered to be recorded.

Court adjourns until Tomorrow 8 oclock.

Wednesday June 17th 1801 Court met according to adjournment Members present (viz) William Walton
    Moses Fisk
    Charles Hudspeth
    James Hibbits and
    Peter Turney, Esquire. Ordered that Leonard Jones be appointed Overseer.
P 40   from the the top of the Ridge between the waters of Paytons & Defeated Creek to Michael Murphys & that Peter Turny Esquire furnish said Overseer with a list of hands.

Ordered that Henry Huddleston be appointed Overseer of the Road from the top of the Ridge, between the waters of Paytons and Defeated Creeks, to the top of the Ridge between the waters of Defeated Creek & Salt Lick Creek, and that all the hands living on Defeated Creek work under said Overseer.

Ordered that Pleasant Kearby be appointed Overseer of the Road from the top of the Ridge between the waters of Defeated & Salt Lick Creeks to the ford of Salt Lick Creek where Keykendalls lives and that all the hands living on Salt Lick Waters, above Kuykendalls work under said Overseer.

Ordered that James Roberts be appointed Overseer of the Road from crossing of Salt Lick at Knykendalls to Fort Blount and that all the hands living on said Creek below said crossing including all the hands on the River above said Creek on the North side of the River up to the mouth of Wartrace Creek work under said Overseer.

Ordered that William Pryor be appointed Overseer of the Road from the head of Snow Creek to Stephen Oldhams, and that William Walton Esquire furnsih said Overseer with a list of hands.

Ordered that Charles Carter be appointed Overseer of the Road lately layed out from William Andersons to Anthony Pates by the way of the great Salt Lick and that all the hands living on the waters of Martins Creek and above the same on the River up to the said Salt Lick work under said Overseer.

Venire Facias to the ensuing Court William Martin Vincient Ridley, Elias Johns, John Gray, Philip Day, Charles McMurry Wm. Hargis Grant Allen, Daniel Mungle, John Brevard Richard Brittain Andrew Greer, Anthony Samuel, James Bradley James Cochran, Josiah Howell, John Shelton, John Johnson, John Douglass, William P 41 Saunders, Henry Dancer Thomas Bowman, Robert Bowman Black Smith, Edward Settles, Daniel Alexander, Charles Smith, Thomas Wimbs, William Gregory, Thomas Sutton, Aaron Hart Edmond Boas, Jeremiah Taylor, Fredrick Debo, William Roper and Isham Beasley.

Ordered that the Report of the Sheriff for non Residents Lands who failed to return the same for Taxation for the year 1800 be received And that the same be Advertised agreeable to Law. which are as follows (viz) John & James Bonner 1854 a acres. Joshua Davis 684 Acres Mame Philips 1240 acres Benjamin Shepphard 3200 acres John P. Williams 1371 acres, John Williams 650 acres, Thomas Shoot(?) 1000 acres, William Wallers 2001 acres, James Armstrong 5000 acres Stephen Pettis 500 acres, Levi West 428 acres Francis Hollenshead - John Drews heirs 1280 acres, Sterling Brewer 640 acres Samuel Saunford 7680 acres, James Adams 640 acres Hiers of James Celton 640 acres Nancy Shepherd 2560 acres William Tyrell 1000 acres Daniel Anderson 640 acres William Shepherk 1350 acres, Robert Thompson 640 acres John Price 640 acres Lardner Clark 64 0 acres, John Kennedy 640 acres John Bartlet 64 0 acres Robert Cartwright 640 acres Thomas Cartwright 640 acres George Cummins 640 acres John Ford 640 acres Heirs of Henry Flury(?) 1000 acres John Gatling 864 acres David Allison 1681 acres Allen Ramsey 1355 acres Edward Yarbrough(?) 3840 acres Captain William Lytle 3000 acres Heirs of Archbald Lytle 3,000 Acres Heirs of John Calloway 640 acres Stephen Cantrill 1000 acres Signed John L. Martin Heirs of Luke Sylvester 640 acres Heirs of Solomon Truit 640 acres Heirs of Joseph Harner 640 acres Heirs of Thomas tentón 640 acres Heirs of John Brabble 640 acres Heirs of Christopher Church 640 acres Heirs of Michael Valuntine 640 acres Heirs of Jas Moore 640 acres Signed   James Gwin.

P 42   It is therefore ordered that the Clerk make out a cretificate of the same together with the amount of the fine taxes and charges due thereon, and cause the same to be twice published in the Knoxville Gazette giving notice that the same will be sold or so much thereof as will satisfy the fine Taxes & costs.

Ordered that Charles Hudspeth Esquire William Martin & Andrew Greer be appointed as inspectors to the insuing Election & that the Sheriff be directed to notify them thereof.

Ordered that William Haynnes Stock Mark a crop & under keel in the right ear & crop & over keel in the left be recorded.

Ordered that Richard Brittain be appointed Overseer of the Road from near Samuel Coruthers at the fork Road up the middle fork of Goose Creek to Daniel Alexanders - And that

Daniel Alexander be appointed Overseer of road leading from his own house to where it intersects the other Road and that James Gwin & James Hibits Esquires furnish said Overseer with a list of hands.

Ordered that John L. Martin be appointed to collect the State & County tax for the present year who gave security and qualified According to Law.

Ordered that Moses Fisk & Garrett Fitsgerald Fitsgerald be appointed to settle with the administrators of William Deceased & report the same to our ensuing Court.

James Roberts Stock mard a crop of the left ear and over slop in the right Ordered to be recorded.

Ordered that Sampson Williams be appointed to survey the land claimed by Seviere & Gordon so as to ascertain Whether Aaron Robins and John Livingston or either of them are on the same and return three Just & fair plans thereof to our next Court Court adjourns till Court in Course to meet at Dixon Springs.

S. Williams

P 43   Monday Dixon Spring September the 21st 1801 - Court met according to adjournment Members present (towit)   Garret Fitzgerald
                                                 Tilman Dixon
                                                 and James Hibits Esquire.

Grand Jurors drawn (viz) John Shelton, James Bradley Richard Brittain, Robert Bowman, Isham Beasley, Charles McMurry, Edmond Boaz, James Cochran Vincient Ridley, Andrew Greer, John Johnson, Elias Johns, John Douglass Foreman, Aaron Hart, Henry Dancer - Daniel Mungle appointed Constable to attend on the Grand Jury and sworn accordingly.

Deed 320 acres Vincient Ridley to Pleasant Emmerson acknowleged and ordered to be registered.

Deed 40 Acres John Murphy to Amos Freeman proven by the oth (oath) of James W. Wright one of the subscribing witnesses Ordered to be Registered.

Robert Bowman Stock mark a crop off the left & a slit in the right ear Ordered to be recorded.

Ordered that William Martins Stock mark be recorded (viz) a cross and under-keel in the right ear and a swallowfork in the left.

Ordered that all persons who have heretofore failed to return lists of ther Taxable property and polls for the present year that the same be received at the present Term.

Daniel Mingle appointed Constable who came into Court gave Security and qualified according to Law.

Deed James Ballow to Godfrey Fowler for 100 acres proven by the oath of Elias Johns one of the subscribing witnesses thereto and ordered to be Registered.

Ordered that Robert Bowman be allowed to build a mill on his own Land on Spring Creek.

P 44   Fredrick Turney(Turner?) stock mark a crop off the right ear ordered to be recorded.

Ordered that Edward Settles be appointed Overseer of the Road where Christian Boston was Overseer and that the same hands work under said Overseer, as worked under said Boston.

Deed 1240 acres Thomas Donoho to Francis Saunders proven by the oath of James Bradley one of the Subscribing Witnesses thereto ordered to be registered.

Ordered that the petition of James & Hannah Snodgras be received and filed of Record.

Deed 640 acres James McKain and Stephen Montgomery to James Montgomery - Acknowleged and ordered to be registered.

Deed 200 acres John Seviers to Edward Irons proven by the oath of George Strother one of the subscribing witnesses ordered to be Registered.

Deed John Seviere to Cornelius Doherty proven by the oath of George Strother one of the subscribing witnesses Ordered to be registered.

Deed of gift Willeroy Pate to Sally Thompson William Thompson Junr. and Robert Thompson Acknowleged and ordered to be Registered.

Court adjourns until tomorrow nine oclock.

Tuesday September 22nd 1801 - Court met according to Adjournment Members present (viz) Garret Fitsgerald Fitsgerald,
Tilman Dixon and
James Hibbits Esquires.

Grant Allens stock mark swallowfork in the right ear and a slit and underkeel in the left - ordered to be recorded.

P 45 Deed Charles Mundine to Abram Moore proven by the oath of John McFarlin one of the Subscribing Witnesses ordered to be Recorded.

Ordered that John Johnson, be appointed Overseer of the Road from Mingles Gap to the County line being the Road that leads to Bledsoes Lick And that James Hibits Esquire furnish said Overseer with a list of hands.

Ordered that John Sutton and Nicholas Darnold be added to William Martins list of hands to work on the Road where he is Overseer.

Ordered that John Johnson be appointed overseer of the Road from Mingles Gap to Dixons Creek at Captain Ballows and that the same hands who worked under John Hargis late overseer work under said Overseer.

Ordered that an Orphan or Foundling Child about seven months old whose name heretofore was unknown but now named Polly Sutton be bound to John Sutton until she arrive to the age of Eighteen years.

Deed 500 acres John Payton to Hugh Stephenson acknowleged & ordered to be Registered.

Ordered that Samuel Stalcup be bound for the maintanance of a Bastard child begotten on the body of Asia Pierce who came into Court and acknowleged himself bond for the maintenance of the same and gave Security according to Law.

Deed for a Town Lot Peter Turney, Tilman Dixon, and William Alexander, to John Ward, was acknowleged by said Dixon & Alexander Ordered to be registered.

Court adjourns until Tomorrow nine oclock.

Wednesday September the 23rd 1801 Court met according to Adjournment Members present (viz) Moses Fisk &
James Hibits Esqr.

P 46 Benjamin Blackburns Stock mark a crop off the left ear and owerbit in the right. And brand the letter B ordered to be Recorded.

Ordered that Tho's Walker be subphoenaed to appear at our next Court to be holden at the Third Monday in December next to shew cause if any he has why David Ventress(Vantrease?) should not be admitted to extend his mill dam across Goose Creek on said Walkers Land.

The Inventory of the Estate of John Burke Dec'd returned into Court by Andrew Greer Administrator.

Ordered that Robert Craggot(?) an Orphan boy about four years old be bound to Benjamin Barton until he attain the age of twentyone, who came into Court and entered into Indentures with William Martin and Basil Shaw his securities.

Ordered that John L. Martin, William L. Alexander Sampson Williams and Thomas Draper be appointed on the Veni fa. to the ensuing Superior Court.

Ordered that Peter Craggot an orphan boy about 10 years old be bound to James Hibits Esquire untill he attain the age of twenty one years.

Venire facias to the ensuing Court (viz) Grant Allen Thomas Jemerson(?) Daniel Mcfarland, James Crerry, Thomas Bowman, Joel Dyer, Edmond Jennings, William Saunders, John Rutherford, John Patterson, William Stalcup James Gibson, William Hargis, John Sedgley, Francis Patterson, Francis Findley, Patrick Donoho, George Tomasson David Ventress Eneas Harrold, William Simpson, William Penny, Josiah Payne, Thos Armstrong Nathaniel Brittin Joel Dyer Sen. John Chambers, Elisha P 47 Oglesby, John Murphy, Michael Murphy, Jeffrey Sutton, Daniel Hammock, Daniel Alexander and Jabez Gifford.

Ordered that Jonas Dancer be allowed a permit to retail whisky at 12½ cents pr half pint for three months he complying with the Requisitions of the law in such case made & provided.

On motion of Samuel Donelson Esquire to have the fine & Double Tax remitted on 500 Acres of Land the property of Stephen Pettis The Court decided that the said motion should lie over until next Court for consideration.

Archebalds Sloans stock mark, a half crop in the left ear and a slit & under bit in the right.

Vincent Ridleys stock mark a half crop in each ear Ordered to be recorded.

Ordered that John Hargis be allowed a permit to retail whisky at 12½ cents he complying with the requisitions of the law in such case made and provided.

Ordered that the following geport be received Benjamin Shepherd 640 acres a lettle below the mouth of Obey on the south side Benjamin Sheppard 640 acres on the Lick Creek, Nancy Shephard 640 acres on the West fork of Roaring River, Do " 640 Joins Do " Do 640 on eastern branch of Roaring River near the head beginning at a Beach & Buckeye entered 18th November 1792 Signed John L. Martin.

Ordered that Sampson Williams be appointed to compleat the survey of the disputed claim between Seviere & Gordon Alexander Suit & others & report the same to our ensuing Court.

P 48 Ordered that Sundry Lands reported by the Sheriff the owner of which has no personal property within this county be certified to the printer of the State for publication being as follows (towit) James Comyns(Cummins?) 1920 in three trachts 640 acres each, James Moores Heirs 1000 acres - Reported Lands (viz) John & James Bonner 64 0 acres on the Ridge between Cumberland & Barren River 3292 acres 738 acres 228 acres & 640 acres. John Armstrong heirs 3840 acres North Side of Cumberland, Joshua Hadley 700 acre s on Paytons Creek. Joshua Davis 1280 acres in two tracts 640 acres each. Jesse Cobb 640 on the waters of Roaring River. Signed John L. Martin.

Court Adjourns until Court in Course to meet at this place &
                                             Sampson Williams.

Dixons Springs December the 21st 1801 - Court met according to adjournment, Members present (viz) Tilman Dixon
                 Peter Turney &
                 James Hibits Esquires.

Bill of sail Samuel Young to James Hibits proven by the oath of Robert Johnson one of the subscribing witnesses.

Deed 65 Acres John Brevard to James Hibits, acknowleged and ordered to be Registered.

Bill of sail James Hibits to John Brevard Acknowleged Ordered to be recorded.

Ordered that Samuel Coruthers, Grant Allen, John Shelton, William Moore, Andrew Greer, William Staloup & James Gibson, be appointed to view, mark, & lay off a Road from Banks ferry to the mouth of the East fork of Goose Creek and report the same to our next Court.

Be it remembered that on the 21st day of December 1801 by virtue of a commission from his Excellency Archibald Roan Esquire of the State of Tennessee be bearing date the 14th day of November 1801 James Roberts, James Draper, William
P 49   Gregory Nathaniel Brittain, John Patterson, Elmore Douglass, Charles Kavanaugh, John Lancaster, William Kavanaugh, Sen., Arthur Hogan, John Looney and Thomas Smith duly commissioned as Justices of the Peace in and for the County Smith came into Court & took the necessary oaths and also the oath of office and took their seals According.

Deed 60 acres Henry Tooley to John White proven by the oath of John Bearkley (Barkley) one of the subscribing witnesses.

Grand Jury drawn, and John Chambers appointed foreman John Chambers foreman, Edmond Jennings, William Penny David Venters, Josiah Payne, Joel Dyer, John Sedgley, Daniel Hammonck, Daniel Alexander, Jeffrey Sutton, William Simpson, Patrick Dohoho , Michael Murphy, Francis Findley, George Tomason.

Court Adjourns until tomorrow nine oclock.

Tuesday the 22nd Court met according to adjournment, Members present, James Hibits,
Elmore Douglass,
John Lancaster,
Williams Kavanaugh,
Nathaniel Brittain and
John Patterson Esqr.

Daniel Alexander is allowed letters of administration to administer on the Estate of Reuben Alexander Deceased who came into Court & qualified and gave Security according to law, and returned an Inventory in Court of said Estate.

Ordered that Sampson Williams be appointed to compleat the Survey claimed by Seviere & Gordon so as to ascertain whether Alexander Suit, Aaron Robins and John Livingston lives upon the same or either of them, that he make said survey agreeable to the directions of both parties and that he returns two just and fair planns thereof into our ensuing Court.

Ordered that Spilsby Coleman be released from paying the Tax on 1000 Acres of
P 50   Land which appears to have been returned or charged to him through mistake, and that the clerk be directed to transmit a copy of this order to the treasurer.

John L. Martin is appointed Sheriff for the ensuing two years who came into Court & gave security & qualified according to law.

Ordered that Rachael Stalcup wife of Samuel Stalcup be cited to appear at next Court to shew cause if any they have why they should not be compelled to give new securities for her Guardianship of her Daughter Dorcass.

Deed 111 acres Griffith Rutherford to Thomas Walker proven by the oath of Francis Look one the subscribing witnesses thereto and ordered to be Registered.

Charles F. Mabias is appointed coroner for two years, who came into Court gave security and qualified according to Law.

Ordered that John Lancaster be allowed letters of administration to administer on the estate of John Lancaster Deceased who gave security & qualified according to Law.

Church Fisher is appointed Constable who came into Court gave security and qualified according to Law.

Silas Jernigan is appointed Constable for two years, who came into Court gave Security and qualified according to Law.

John Kavanaugh is appointed Constable for two years who came into Court gave Security and qualified according to Law.

Daniel Draper is appointed Constable who came into Court gave Security and qualified according to Law.

Ordered that the Settlement of the Estate Cain Acuff be recieved and entered of Record.

P 51   Deed 140 acres Peter Turney to Lewis Smith proven by the oath of Landy Shoemake one of the subscribing witnesses Ordered to be registered.

Deed 450 acres Henry W. Lawson to Lewis Corder proven by the oath of Willis Jones one of the subscribing witnesses Ordered to be Registered.

Court Adjourns until Tomorrow nine oclock.

Wednesday December the 23rd Court met according to adjournment Members present (viz) Charles Kavanaugh
  John Lancaster
  Elmore Douglass,
  Williams Kavanaugh &
  Arthur Hogan Esq.

John Carter, who appears to have been subpoenaed at the Instance of Alexander Suit: in the suit John Seviere & George Gordon against him, being called, failed to appear. Whereupon the Court ordered that he be called out on his subpoena, and that Scirefacias Issue against him agreeable to Law.

James Gwin is appointed County Trustee who came into Court give security and qualified according to Law.

Robert Cotton is appointed Constable who came into Court and gave Security & qualified according to Law.

Stephen Copeland, John Payton, John Fitsgerald and James Taylor is appointed a Jury to view by the assent of parties in the case of Seviere & Gordon against

Alexander Suit Aron Robins and John Livingston to meet on the premises at such time & place as the Surveyor may appoint.

Court Adjourns until tomorrow nine oclock.

Tuesday November the 24th Court met according to adjournment, Members present,
Tilman Dixon
John Lancaster
Arthur Hogan and
Williams Kavanaugh Esquires Gentlemen.

Charles Kavanaugh is appointed Overseer of the Road from the head of Walkers Creek, to Charles Kavanaugh Esquires plantation and that the hands who usually
P 52   worked on the said Road work under him.

Ordered that Elijah Gaddi be appointed Overseer of the road from the cross roads at Esquire Kavanaugh plantation to where the County line crosses the Nashville road and that the same hands work under him as usually did.

Silas Jernigan has resigned his appointement as Overseer of the road leading from Dixons Lick to Peter Turneys & Alexander Ferrell is appointed Overseer in his place and the same hands to work under him as worked under the late Overseer.

John(Joseph?) Bishop is appointed Overseer of the road from Bishops Ferry to the cross roads leading from the Round Lick to Nashville & that Elmore Douglass & Williams Kavanaugh furnish said Overseer with a list of hands.

James Rother is appointed Overseer of the Road from the crossroads to Williams Kavanaughs Esquire and that the same men furnish said Overseer with a list of hands as above.

John Capinger(Caplinger?) is appointed Overseer of the road leading from Hickmans Creek from Williams Kavanaughs Esquire to a spring about a mile north from James Kitchens and that the same hands work under said Overseer as usually worked on said Road.

James Kittchin is appointed Overseer of the Road from his own house to Charles Kavanaughs Esquire and that the same hands as usually worked on said Road, work under s'd Overseer.

Thomas Banks is appointed Overseer of the Bledsoesborough road to the County line and that Elmore Douglass and Williams Kavanaugh Esquires furnish said Overseer with a list of hands.

Colo. William Martin is appointed Overseer of the Road from the ford of Dixons
P 53   Creek to Peter Turneys Esquire and that all the hands above said Road work under him.

Arthur Hogan Esquire is appointed Overseer of the road from the mouth of Caney fork, towards Creek and that all the hands that formerly worked on said road work under him.

Silas Rolls is appointed Overseer of the road from Wards Creek to Round Lick Creek, and that the same hands as usually worked on said road work under said Overseer.

Armistead Moore is appointed Overseer of the Road from round Lick to the County line and that the same hands work under said Overseer as usually worked on said Road.

Ordered that Thomas Banks, Daniel Burford, William Thompson Jones Bishop, Silas Rolls, Samuel King & William Hankins be appointed as a Jury to view mark & lay off a road from Banks ferry, to intersect the Road that leads to Williams Kavanaughs and that they report the same to our ensuing Court.

Ordered that Nathaniel Farrier, Joseph Jordan, Richard Cantrill Larkin Bethel, Daniel Allen Henry Hays and Jacob Turney view mark & lay off a Road from John Looneys Esq. to Esquire Kavanaugh and that they report the same to our ensuing County Court.

Charles Kavanaugh Esquire is allowed a tavern Licence to keep an ordinary at his now dwelling house and that he be rated agreeable to the common rates of this Country & gave security accordingly.

Venire faceas to the ensuing Court Robert Dugan, James Baker, Hesikiah, Woodard, Wm.Payne, Armistead Moore George Rooling Thomas Walker, John Rutherford, Daniel Hitton, Richard Lancaster, Leonard Fight, Willeroy Pate, Nathan Ridley, Pleasant Kearby, James Wray Michael Murphy, Willie Sullivan, William Pryor, P 54   William Epperson, Samuel Stalcup Big. Joel Dyer, William Kelton, Joel Hallum Josiah Howell Stephen Montgomery, David Keilough Senr. Jeremiah Taylor, James Bradley, David Keilough Junr. Vincient Ridley, Godfrey, Henry King, Aaron Hart, Henry Dancer, Benjamin Johns, and James W. wright.

Ordered that Thomas Stewart Esquire be allowed to return 640 acres of originally David Allisons and purchased by him at Sheriff Sail in summer - And the tax was paid accordingly for the year Eighteen Hundred and one.

Ordered that John L. Martin Esquire be allowed 45 dollars for his Exoficio Services as Sheriff the proceeding year.

Ordered that Joel Dyer be released from working on the Fort Blount Road.

Court Adjourns until Court in course to meet at the house of Colo. William Saunders.
Test   William Walton
Sampson Williams   James Hibits
                                       Arthur Hogan

March Term 1802 At a Court opened and held at the late dwelling house of William Saunders, on Monday the 15th of March 1802 Members present (viz) William Walton Peter Turney
        Elmore Douglass
        Williams Kavanaugh,
        James Hibbits and
        John Lancaster Esquires.

Ordered that Daniel Alexander be allowed a retailing Licence to keep Tavern at his now dwelling house & that he be rated as follows (towit) for breakfast, Dinner & Supper 25 cents for whisky by the half pint 12½ cents for Brandy 12½ cents for lodging 6¼ cents for stabling & forrage twelve 25 cents For corn or P 55   oats pr. half gallon 6¼ cents who came into Court and gave Security according to Law.

Bill of sail Sampson Williams to William Marchbanks Acknowleged & ordered to be recorded.

The following Gentlemen were impanneled Elected & sworn as Grand Jurors (viz) Stephen Montgomery foreman James Bradley, James W. Wright, Michael Murphy, Robert Dugan, Hesakiah Woodward, Jeremiah Taylor, Vincient Ridley, Thomas Walker, Leonard Fight Samuel Stalcup, Nathaniel Ridley and James Baker who were charged and sent out to inquire of Indictments &c and Robert Cotton was appointed Constable to attent them.

Deed 254 acres William Walton to Richard Taylor Acknowleged & ordered to be registered.

Deed 50 acres Charles F. Mabias to Philip Day, acknowleged and ordered to be Registered.

Richard Clarks Stock mark a crop off the right & a swallow fork & an under bit in the left, Ordered to be recorded.

Deed Zachariah Green (or possibly Greer?) & William Gillispie, to Roderick Jenkins proven by the Oath of Robert Collier one of the subscribing witnesses thereto & ordered to be recorded.

Deed 100 acres Roderick Jinkins to William Jinkins acknowleged.

Deed Thomas Stokes to Jones Bishop 100 acres proven by the oath of Willis Jones one of the subscribing witnesses thereto.

Ordered that John Simpson, who is charged with begetting a Bastard child upon the body of Elizabeth Wakefield be fined according to law. And that he be bound in a recognizance in the sum of three hundred dollars with James Simpson and Roderick Jenkins his securities, to be void on condition that the John Simpson P 54(a) indemnifies the county as to the maintenance of said child & perform such order as said Court may from time to time make concerning the same.

Deed 360 acres Robert Fenner to John Burris proven by the oath of James Blackburn one of the subscribing witnesses thereto.

Ordered that the resignation of John L. Martin Esquire as Sheriff be received he having tendered the same in open Court and that Silas Jernigan Esquire be appointed Sheriff protem.

Ordered that William Martin be allowed to inter into bond & Security for his performance as surveyor of the County of Smith who produced his commission from the Governor bearing date the 27th day of November 1801 and took the following oath I William Martin do swear that I will well and truly perform all the duties of county Surveyor in the County of Smith to the best of my knowlege & belief and that I will only take my Lawful fees, So help me God & his saints.

Test   Sampson Williams   Signed   William Martin

Court Adjourns until tomorrow nine oclock.

Tuesday March the 16th 1802 Court met according to adjournment Members present (viz) Elmore Douglass
          Williams Kavanaugh and
          John Lancaster Esquires.

Deed 500 Acres Hugh Stephenson to Thomas Harrison proven by the oath of John Wilson one of the subscribing witnesses.

Deed 560 acres Thomas Harrison & Thomas Huchinson to John Wilson proven by the oath of William Huchinson one of the Subscribing witnesses thereto Ordered to be Registered.

Ordered that John Morris charged by Polly Payne with begetting of a Bastard P 55(a)   child upon her body be bound in recognizance in the sum of three hundred dollars whereupon the said John Morris came into ?Court and acknowleged himself indebted to the Justices of the County Court of Smith and their successors in office in the aforesaid sum of three hundred dollars with William Hayne and Charles McMurry his securities to be void on condition that the afforesaid John Morris doth keep the said County of Smith indemmified as to the maintenance of said child and perform such other orders as the said Court may from time to time make concerning the same and the said William Haynie & Charles McMurry came into Court and acknowleged themselves securities for the said John Morris's performance of the above Recognizance.

Ordered that John Morris & Polley Payne be fined twenty five shillings each Proclamation money for the crime of fornication and costs which was immediately paid into Court.

Deed 260 Acres Richard Banks to George Bradley acknowleged in open Court and ordered to be Registered.

Ordered that Lee Sullivan be allowed to qualify as a a Justice of Peace who came into Court and took the necessary oaths & the oath of office and took his seat accordingly.

James W. Wrights Stock mark a half crop out of the under side of the left ear and a slit in the right ordered to be Recorded.

Deed 365 Acres William Saunders to James Fedlock(?) proven by the oath of John Wilson and Williams Hutchinson the subscribing witnesses thereto Ordered to be registered.

Deed 160 Acres Lee Sullivan to William acknowleged.

Nathaniel Ridleys Stock mark a crop off the right ear & a crop & a slit in the left ordered to be recorded.

P 56   Ordered John Morris pay instantly to Polly Payne the sum of ten dollars for the maintenance of a child begotten by said Morris on the body of the said Polley Payne and that he remain in custody of the Sheriff until paid.

Ordered that the inventory account of Sales of the Estate of John Lee deceased returned into Court & ordered to be filed of Record.

Deed 346 acres Thomas Stokes to Boling Felts proven by the oath of Stephen Robertson one of the subscribing witnesses thereto and ordered to be Registered

Ordered that Elias Johns be allowed to keep a ferry at the upper end of the first Bluff below the mouth of Paytons Creek and that he be rated as follows (viz) for each man & Horse 12½ cents for each Single man or horse 6¼ cents for each Pack Horse 12½ cents for each head of horned cattle 6¼ for all other Stock two cents who came into Court and gave Security accordingly.

Ordered that a tract of Land said to be reported of four hundred & twenty eight acres lying on the middle fork of the East fork of Goose Creek in the name of John & James Bonner be remitted on paying the usual Tax & incidental costs.

Deed 103 acres Joshua Hadley to James Dobins proven by the oath of Micham Smith one of the subscribing witnesses.

Deed 100 acres Joshua Hadley to Hugh McKennish proven by the oath of Micham Smith one of the Subscribing witnesses thereto Ordered to be registered.

Ordered that a public Road be viewed marked & layed off from Dixons Spring the nearest & best way crossing Cumberland River at the uper end of the Bluff below

the mouth of Paytons Creek on the South side of said River to intersect the road
leading to Smiths fork at the most convenient Place, and that edmond Jennings, Thomas
Jameson, Elias Johns Thomas Gosset(or Garset?) and Lewis Macfarland view the same
& make report the same to our next Court.

Deed 320 acres William Holliday to Willeroy Pate proven by the oath of Landy
Shoemake one of the subscribing witnesses thereto.

Ordered that William Richards Moses Ashbrooks William Walton Charles McClennen,
Charles Mundine, William Holliday and William Sullivan view, mark & lay off a
road from Captain Paits on the Fort Blount road, to Bowmans Mill on (and?) Spring
& that they report the same to our next Court.

David White who appears to be duly commissioned as a Justice of the Peace
for the County of Smith came into Court & qualified according to Law.

Ordered that Michael Osturn have a Tavern License to keep an ordinary at his
now dwelling house and that he be rated agreeable to the costomary rates of retailors in Smith County, who came into Court & gave Security accordingly.

Ordered that Richard Lancaster & Thomas Lancaster William Pryor, James Pryor,
William Walker, John Goad and David Morrison view mark & lay off a road from Lancasters ferry on Caney fork to intersect Waltons road at the most convenient going
towards Knoxville.

In the Ejectment Gordon & Seviere vs Alexander Suit, order to take the depositions of William White north Carolina 30 days notice to be given the Plaintiff.

Ordered that William Haynie, and John Crosswhite, be relased from their
Securityship, for Rachael Clark now Rachael Staloup for their Daughter Dorcass from
P 58 Daughter Dorcass from the commencement thereof and that Samuel Staloup be
appointed Guardian for the said Dorcass Clark, who gave Daniel Mcfarland & Richard
Clark his securities who came into Court & were approved of.

Edward Cage Stock mark, an under keel in each ear, Ordered to be Recorded.

Ordered that an Election be held for Sheriff, whereupon the Court made choice
of John Douglass unanimously whereupon the said John Douglass came into Court &
gave Security and Qualified according to Law.

Ordered that John Lawrence be allowed to return 1000 acres of Land for taxation, for the year 1801 lying at the Junction of the Caney Fork with Cumberland
and in the forks thereof.

Ordered that Isaac Walton be allowed to return 960 acres of Land entered in
his own & more Stephensons names for Taxation in the year 1801.

Thomas Walker who was cited to the present Term by David Ventress to Shew
why the said David Ventress should not extend Mill Dam across Goose Creek on the
Lands of the said Thomas Walker, who came into Court & gave Satisfactory Reasons,
why the said Mill Dam should not be extended as aforesaid and the Said Court directed that the said Thomas Walker should be discharged from further attendance
and that the Said David Ventress should pay all costs of Such Citation.

Henry Tooley Stock mark, a swallow fork, in the right ear and a cross & under
bitt in the left - To be recorded, &C.

Ordered that Elmore Douglass Esquire take in the list of Taxable property
& Polls for Cap Bishops Company William Kavanaugh Esquire for Captain Moores
P 59 Company, Thomas Smith for Capt. Lancasters Company, John Looney Esq. for

Cap Kavanaughs Company Lee Sullivan Esqr. for Cap. Pryors Company John Patterson
for his own Company, Nathaniel Brittain for Cap. Griffords Company, David White
Esquire, Capt Caseys Company, Peter Turney Esq. Capt. Bellows Company, William
Gregory Cap Settles Company, James Roberts Esq. Cap. Pates Company and James Draper
Esquire for Jennings Creek & Baren Waters And such list so taken return into our
ensuing Court.

Ordered that Richard Taylor be appointed Overseer of the road from the ford
of Paytons Creek to the top of the sideling hill between that & Waltons ferry,
and that all hands belonging to that part of said who were liable to work under
William Walton shall work on the same.

The Court adjourned until Tomorrow nine Oclock.

Wednesday March the 17th 1802, Members present Elmore Douglass
                                    Williams Kavanaugh &
                                    Charles Kavanaugh Esqrs.

Deed 366 acres Josiah Reditt to Peter Turney proven by the Oath of James Bellows
one of the Subscribing witnesses thereto.

Deed from M. Phillips to James Bellew 640 acres proven by the oath of Peter
Turney one of the subscribing witnesses thereto.

Deed 6 Acres John Fisher to Dempsey Kenedy one of the subscribbing witnesses
thereto & Ordered to be Registered.

Ordered that William Saunders be allowed letters of administration on the
Estate of Bennet Rogers Deceasd. who came into Court and gave security & qualified
according to Law.

Ordered that John L. Martin late Sheriff of Smith County be allowed the sum
of eight dollars for his exofficio services from the last to the present term.

P 60   Ordered that Charles F. Mabias coroner be allowed the sum of one dollar
for his exofficio Services for Summoning the Venire to the Superior Court for the
last Term.

Ordered that Leonard Fight be appointed Overseer of the road from the head
of Walkers Creek to Lancasters Mill and that all the hands who worked on Said Road
in the Same bounds by Order of Wilson Court also Work on the Same.

Ordered that Richard Lancaster be appointed Overseer of the road from Lancasters Mill to Caney fork, and that the same hands that worked by Order of Wilson
Court and in the Same bounds work on the same.

Brittain vs Christian De.P. for the Plaintiff, Devan(?) Kentucky 30 days notice.

Ordered that William Saunders, William Gregory John Jamison, be appointed a
jury to view mark & lay off a determine whether the Road leading from Dixon Springs
to Caney Fork can be turned so as to go above or below Robert Bowmans Mill and
make report thereof to our ensuing County Court.

Robert Dugans Stock mark a crop off the left ear and a half crop in the under
side of the right ear Ordered to be Recorded.

Elmore Douglass Stock mark is an under & over bit in each ear and Stock
brand the letter E Ordered to be recorded.

Zadock B. Thackstons Stock mark is a is two overkeels and two crops one in each ear Ordered to be recorded.

Hesekiahs Stock mark is a swallowford in the right & a crop off the left Ordered to be recorded.

James Bradleys mark is a crop and slit in each ear & Brand with the figure
P 61 3 and letter B Ordered to be Recorded.

John Sittons Stock mark is a crop & a corner Slit in the right ear and a swallow fork and under bit in the left and Brand is a Roman J. S. Ordered to be recorded.

James Doherty vs Hesekiah Oneal, Ordered that in this case the De Po. of Absolem Hooper be taken at the house of William Donelson Esquire de bene esse to be read in Evidence in this case, notice served or acknowleged by Plff. Council Depo. to be taken the first of June next.

Thomace Wallace vs Daniel Zimmerman(?) De Po. to Issue to take the Deposition of Charles Ca rr, in the State of Kentucky at the house of James Morrison or Henry Clay to be taken at the instance of the Plaintiff 30 days notice, given given the Deft attorney Shall be considered legal notice notice notice to the Defendant.

Willis Jones Stock mark is an under Slope in the right ear & half crop in the left. Ordered to be recorded.

Richard Banks stock mark an under keel in the right & over keel in the left ear, Ordered to be Recorded.

Ordered that a Public road be established from Docton Mabias to Dixons Still House as Doctor Mabias is willing to open the same at his own expense.

Ordered that Armistead Moore, William Hankins Harris Bradford, Jones Bishop, Joseph Bishop William Thompson Daniel Burford Junr. and Moses Evans be appointed a Jury to view mark & lay off a road from Richard Banks ferry the nearest and best way to fall Creek & from thence to view & return the old road leading from Bishops ferry up the Round Lick and to intersect a new road at the most convenient place at or near William Kavanaugh.

Samuel Evits stock mark is two slits in the right ear and a slit & under bit in the left is exhibited to be Recorded &c.

Tuesday March the 18th 1802 - Court met according to adjournment Members present, :viz: Peter Turney,
P 62   Elmore Douglass
            Charles Kavanaugh
            Williams Kavanaugh and
            John Lancaster Esqr.

Venire facias for the Superior Court, Charles Kavanaugh Peter Turney, James Wright & James Ballow.

Ordered that the inventory account of the Estate of John Lancaster Deceased be received and entered of record.

Isham Beazley exhibited his Stock mark being a crop & half crop in the left ear & a half crop in the right, Ordered to be recorded.

James Wright Exhibited his Stock mark being a crop & half crop in each ear, under in the right & over in the left & brand O ordered to be recorded.

Charles Kavanaugh Exhibited his Stock mark being a crop and slit in the right ear & crop and under keel in the left ordered to be recorded.

James Ballow Exhibited his stock mark being a crop, and two slits in the right ear & a crop off the left and Brand J. B. ordered to be recorded.

Williams Kavanaugh Exhibited his stock mark being a crop & under keel in the left ear and a half crop in the right ear Ordered to be Recorded.

Venire facias for the ensuing County Court, Edward Cage, Lewis Smith, Zaddock B Thackston, Samuel King, Robert Ward, Leonard Ballow, Benjamin Barton Isham Beasley, William Hargis, James Cherry, Charles McMurry, Abraham Brittain, Willeroy Pate, Henry Huddleston, William Marchbanks, Joseph Williamson, Willie Sullivan, Thomas Heaton, Robert Rowland, Andrew Greer, Henry Dancer, John Brevard, John Grey, Daniel Hammock, John Barkley, William Penny, John Kearby, William Stalcup, Patrick Donoho, Patrick Donoho, Francis Patterson, William Payne, Moses Pinkston P 62 (a) Reuben Goard John Chambers Senr. Thomas Jamison and Edward Farris.

Ordered that Moses Fisk, Peter Turney, & Garrett Fitsgerald or any two of them, be authorised to compleat a settlement with the Administrator and Administratrix of the Estate of William Young Deceased and suhh Settlement when compleated to return into Court with the vouchers relative thereto.

Bill of Sail Samuel Parker to William White being certified by Nathaniel Lane Clerk of Wake County & attested by two of the Justices of the Peace for the same as having been acknowleged before them. Ordered to be recorded.

Ordered that the report of a road from John Looney to Charles Kavanaughs be received. And that Nathaniel Farrier and William Madin be appointed to open & keep the same in repair each Overseer to meet at Richard Cantrills and that John Looney Esquire furnish them with a list of hands.

John Douglass Esquire protests against the Jail of Smith County and the Court ordered it it be Recorded.

Ordered that all the hands liable to work on public roads and living on the waters of Mulherins Creek work under James Kitchin.

Court Adjourns until Court in course to meet at this place
Attest   Peter Turney
Sampson Williams   John Lancaster
                                          Elmore Douglass

June Term 1802. At a Court opened & held for the County of Smith at William Saunders on Monday the 21st day of June 1802. Present Peter Turney
                                          Nathaniel Brittain
                                          Elmore Douglass, and
                                          John Looney Esquires.

The Court then proceeded to business, and appointed Reuben Goad who came into P 63 Court gave Security & Quallified according to Law.

Ordered that James Dobbins be allowed to build a Grist Mill on his own land upon Paytons Creek.

Ordered that John Kearby be exempted from serving on the Venire at this Term.

Grand Jury drawn (viz) John Bearkley(Barkley?) foreman Thomas Jamerson, William Penny, William Stalcup, John Gray, Patrick Donoho, Abraham Brittain, Daniel Hammock, Robert Roaland, William Payne, Charles McMurry, John Chambers, who were impaneld charged & sworn, & Thos. Wright appointed Constable to attend them.

Deed 300 Acres James Montgomery to John Kenedy proven by the oath of Dempsy Canedy a subscribing witness thereto.

Deed 20 acres John L. Martin to Wm. Alexander proven by the oath of David Cochran one of the subscribing witnesses thereto & ordered to be Registered.

Deed 100 acres Thomas & Mourning White to Richard Pryor proven by the Oath of William Pryor one of the Subscribing Witness.

Deed 320 Acres Duncan Stewart to Robert Bowman proven by the oath of John Chambers one of the Subscribing Witnesses thereto & ordered to be Registered.

Ordered that the Inventory account of the Sails of the Estate of Reuben Alexander deceasd. be received & entered of Record.

Ordered that William Fisher & Freeman Burrow be appointed Constables who came into Court gave Security & quallified According to Law.

Deed 320 acres Duncan Stuart to John Chambers proven by the oath of Robert Bowman one of the Subscribing witnesses.

P 64   Ordered that a road be layed off agreeable to Law from the Jackson County line to cross Cumberland at or near the mouth of Wartrace Creek to intersect the road that leads up Salt Lick Creek to Wakefields at the most convenient place. And that James Draper, Eson Graves, Jacob Jenkins, James Wray Junr. Sampson Williams & Thomas Draper be a Jury to view the same & make report thereof to our ensuing Court.

Ordered that James Wray be allowed to keep a ferry at the mouth of Wartrace Creek on Cumberland River and that he be allowed the sum of 12½ cents for each man & horse, 6¼ cents for a single man or single horse 12½ cents for a pack horse & for each head of horned cattle 6¼ cents & for all other live Stock 2 cents for each Waggon & team 1 dollar for each Cart & team 50 cents for each four wheel carriage of pleasure for the conveyance of persons one Dollar for each two wheel Carriage Ditto 50 cents who came into Court and gave Security according to Law.

Ordered that Samuel Stalcup be allowed a Licence to keep an Ordinary at his now dwelling house on Paytons Creek and that he be rated agreeable to the customary rates of all other Taverns in this County who came into Court ang gave Security accordingly.

Deed 75 acres William Haynie to Elijah Haynie. Acknowleged and Ordered to be registered.

Ordered that Daniel Witcher, Reuben Goad James Bodine Martin Young, Absalem Tedwell, Charles Wakefield, James McKain Willoughby Pugh, William Jenkins, Robert Collier Frederick Hill and Louis Pepkin be a Jury to view mark & lay off a road agreeable to law, from Daniel Witchers to the State line on a direction to the Salt Petre Cave and report the same to our next Court.

Ordered that Thomas Draper be Overseer of the road from Pleasant Kearby to P 65   Daniel Witchers and that all the hands living on Wartrace waters and on the main fork of Salt Lick Creek and the waters thereof, work under said Overseer.

Ordered that the Certificate of Governor Williams of North Carolina and als the Certificate of William White Secretary of said State with the papers accompanying the Same, in Favor of Joseph Fox be admitted to record & that the same be registered.

Ordered that Andrew Greer, William Coruthers William Martin & Peter Turney, James Ballow Daniel Tyree Godfrey Fowler William Douglass Vincent Ridley and Abram Thompson be Jury to lay off & mark a road from Samuel Coruthers to intersect the Fort Blount Road near McFarland.

Ordered that Robert Collier be Overseer of the road from Michael Murphy's to Witchers on the ridge & that Martin Young, Tandy Witcher, Absalem Tedwell Jonathan Hill William Tedwell Charles Wakefield Junr. William Marshal Lucy Witcher, Daniel Witcher, Charles Wakefield Sen. James Bodine Reubin Goad William Jenkins William Donoho Frederick Jones, James McKain George Wins and(or Winzand?) work under him.

Ordered that Stephen Box be Overseer of that part of the road that leads down long Creek beginning at the foot of the ridge the old way from thence down the Creek to the forks of the Road and that Thomas Wimbs, George Sadler, Nathan Dillon, Isaac Dillon, Henry Boaz, John Barth, John Buttoon, David Cooper, Meredith Helms, David Jennings, John Cooper Joseph Strain, William Denny, Eli Pitford, Daniel Pitford, Levi Tedjel(?) James Gwin & Owen Stratton work under him.

P 66   Ordered that George Anderson be Overseer of the Road from the forks of the Road on long Creek to the State line and that John Fisher, William Fisher, William Bartlet, Nathan Bartlet Samuel White, Robert McKinley, Ezekield Wray, Daniel Bridgman, Leroy Casey, Joseph, Dempsy Kenedy, John Nicholas, Stephen Montgomery, John Smith, Michael Neere(?) and Thomas McFarren work under him.

Ordered that Daniel Alexander be Overseer where he is now Overseer, and that James Montgomery, John Kenedy, Joel Holland, Josiah Howell William Cross, Owen Sullivan Isaac Sullivan, Daniel Sullivan, Hugh Larimore, Joseph Sullivan and Andrew Golbfeath, Jacob Kenedy, William Hellums, Hugh Stephenson, William Malone, Richard Bowen, Elisha Oglesby, Robert Moffit, and Roah Eddy work under said Overseer.

Ordered that Burrell Drewer, Stephen Robertson, Josiah Reynolds, Henry Moore Junr. Charles Kavanaugh Esquire Thomas Flood & Cap Charles Kavanaugh, be a Jury to view mark & lay off a road from Bowlings Felts(or Pitts?) on Smiths fork to intersect the Nashville road at the most convenient place for the upper settlement of Hickmans Creek and that they report the same to our next Court.

Deed 345½ Acres George Laurence to Joseph Laurence proven by the Oath of Adam Laurnece one of the subscribing witnesses thereto & Ordered to be Recorded.

Deed 200 Acres Thomas & Morning White To James Ewing proven by the oath of William Pryor one of the subscribing witnesses thereto. Ordered to Registered.

Court Adjourns until tomorrow nine oclock.

P 67   Tuesday June the 22nd 1802 Court met according to adjournment Members present James Gwin,
    Elmore Douglass
    John Looney and
    Williams Kavanaugh Esquires.

Deed 100 Acres Charles Kavanaugh to William Neal Ackd.

Deed Thomas Hickman to Henry Moore proven by the oath of Charles Kavanaugh Esqr. one of the subscribing witnesses.

Deed 100 Acres Thomas Hickman to George Tinkle proven by the oaths of Charles Kavanaugh Esqr. one of the subscribing witnesses.

Deed 200 Acres John Barker to William Neel proven by the oath of Charles Kavanaugh Esqr. one of the subscribing witnesses.

Deed 200 Acres John Irwin to Joel Holland proven by the oath of James Gwin one of the Subscribing witnesses thereto.

Deed Henry Tooley to John Barkley 328 acres Acknowleged.

Deed 10 acres Henry Tooley John Barkley acknowleged.

Peter Turney Esquire produced a commission from his Excellency Governor Roan wherein the said Turney is appointed Entry Taker protempore who gave Security and took the following Oath :viz: I Peter Turney do Swear that I will well & truly perform all the duties of Entry Taker in & for the County of Smith agreeable to Law during my continuance in Office to the best of my Knowlege and belief. Attest Sampson Williams.   Peter Turney

Ordered that the Grand Jury be discharged from further attendance at this Term.

The Court agrees to adjourn this Court to meet at the dwelling house of William Walton at their next term & ordered the same to be entered of Record.

P 68   Ordered that a County tax of 6½ cents belaid on each 100 acres of land, a Tax of 6½ cents on each poll, and a tax of 25 cents on each Stud Horse To be layed for the present year.

Court Adjourns until tomorrow nien oclock.

Wednesday June the 23rd 1802 Court met according to adjournment Members present (towit) James Gwin,
                James Hibits
                Elmore Douglass
                Charles Kavanaugh &
                Williams Kavanaugh Esquire.

Ordered that the Inventory account of the Estate of Bennett Rogers decd. returned into Court by William Saunders Administrator be recieved and ordered to be Recorded.

Deed 100 Acres Jacob Hawick to John Lovelady acknowleged and ordered to be registered.

Deed 100 Acres Ammon Davis to Jacob Hawick proven by the oath of William Martin one of the subscribing witnesses thereto.

Ordered that Daniel Mingle be Overseer of the road from the forks above Samuel Curothers to Daniel Alexanders and that the same hands work under him, as worked under Richard Brittain late Overseer.

Ordered that the late amendment made on the Road from Charles Kavanaughs towards Nashville as far as the Wilson line be established as the public Road and that Elijah Gadda be Overseer of the same and that the same hands work under him as did by order of Wilson Court.

Ordered that John Gordon William Hughs, John Haney, William Smith, Mathew Payne Jessee Smith and Thomas Lancaster be a Jury to view mark & lay off a Road agreeable to Law from Waltons ferry to Lancasters Mill.

Ordered that John Campbell, Joseph Collins Zaddock McNew Isaac Moore, Robert Smith Zachariah Ford, and Ennis(?) Harrold be a Jury to view mark & lay off a road from Charles Kavanaughs down Hickmans Creek passing Josep Collins' to a certain ford near Thomas Smiths and from thence the nearest and best way to intersect Waltons Road at the most convinent place.

P 69

Ordered that Archibald Sloan be Overseer of the road from Michael Murphys to the top of the Ridge between Paytons & Defeated Creeks and that all the hands living on the fork of the road leads up, including Michael Murphy's hands & all the hands on the fork George Thompson lives on and the fork William Kelton lives on, and the fork said Sloan lives on from his own house down to said road work under said Overseer.

Ordered that Lewis Mcfarland be allowed the sum of twenty-eight dollars in full compensation for his services for twenty eight days labor in marking the County line as provided by act of Assembly and that the same be paid out of any County monies in the hands of the County Trustee.

Ordered that Willis Jones be allowed the sum of fifty six dollars as Surveyor for running the boundary lines between the Counties of Smith & Wilson, an also between Smith & Jackson Counties as provided by act of Assembly.

Bill of Sail John L. Martin as Sheriff to Sampson Williams Acknoweged & Ordered to be registered.

Deed 320 Acres Lemuel Hogan to David Hodges proven by the oath of John Ward one of the subscribing witnesses.

Seviers & Gordon vs John Din(?) & Aaron Robbins De Po to issue for the Deft. to take the Deposition of William White of North Carolina & Archibald Roan Esqr. Gov. &C. 30 days notice to be given the Plff. in takin the Deposition of White, & twenty days in taking the deposition of Governor Roan.

The Same Order as above in the Suit Seviere & Gordon vs Alexander Suit.

P 70   Court Adjourns until Tomorrow nine oclock.

Thursday June the 24th 1802 Court met according to adjournment Members present (viz) James Gwin
     Elmore Douglass &
     Williams Kavanaugh Esquires.

Ordered that the corn levied upon by the Constable, be sold agreeable to Law, and that the monies arrising therefrom be deposited in the Clerks Office.

Ordered that Armistead Moore, Joel Holland, Richard Lancaster William Pryor, George Roland, David Keilough, Godfrey Fowler David Keilough Senr. & Henry King be released from the Scire facias the State vs them for their non attendance as Jurors at March Term last.

Ordered that Willeroy Pate & Willie Sullivan each be fined according to act of Assembly for their non attendance as Jurors at March term last, subject neverthe-less to give in their reasons for their non attendance as aforesaid until next Court, and that Scire facias issue against Josiah Howell, and Aaron Hart for their nonattentance as afsd.

Venire Facias— John Gordon, Joel Holland, Dempsey Kenedy, William Stephenson, William Thompson, John Poe, Joseph Berry, Daniel Kavanaugh, John War, William Wooten, Philip Sutton, Vincent Ridley, Jeffrey Sutton William Vordine, Allen Wilkinson, William Kelton, George Thomason, Alexander Piper, Samuel Stalcup Thomas Lancaster Boling Felts, Isaac Johns John Shelton, William Lancaster, Masurces Cotton John Fite, Henry Moore, Joseph Collens William Shaw, Charles

McClennen Grant Allen, Anthony Samuel James Bradley William L. Alexander Junr.
James Stephens John Cooper.

P 69(A)   Ordered that Joel Holland & Josiah Howell be appraisors for Cap.
Caseys Company to value property under Execution William L. Alexander and James
Ballow for Cap. Ballows company, Henry Moore Cap. Kavanaughs Company, Stephen
Robinson & William Lancaster for Cap. Fites Company, Andrew Greer & Richard Brit-
tain for Captain Giffords Company Benjamin Clark & William Thompson for Cap Bishops
Company, Armistead Moore and Williams Kavanaugh for Cap Moores Company Grant Allen
& John Shelton for Cap. Pattersons Company for the purpose of valueing property
taken under Execution, where the Original Contract was for property.

John Douglass Esqr. Sheriff is appointed Collector of the State and County
Tax for the year 1802 who came into Court gave Security and quallified according
to law.

Ordered that James Vance be Overseer of the Road from John Lancasters ferry
to Waltons road & that John Lancaster Esqr. furnish said Overseer with a list of
hands.

Ordered that Wilson Cage, James Bradley & Andrew Greer be commissioners to
divide the tract of Land whereon Michael Murphy lives, between the heirs of William
Young Deceasd. agreeable to Law & also that they lay off one third of the said
tract to the widow of the said Deceased to include his mansion house.

Ordered that the account & vouchers allowed by Moses Fisk & Peter Turney
Esquires in the settlement by them mad with the administratrix & Administrator be
received and the settlement entered of Record.

Letter of Attorney Joshua Knowlton to Sampson proven proven by the oath of
Archibald Sloane a subscribing Witness thereto.

P 70(A)   Ordered that John Rankins be Overseer of the road where Frederick Debo
was Overseer and that the same hands work under him.

Ordered that Josiah Payne be Overseer of the Road from Dixons Springs, to
the ford of Dixons Creek on the Fort Blount road and the same hands work under him
as were liable to work under the late Overseer.

Ordered that Henry Tooley be Overseer of that part of the road where Robert
Bowman was Overseer & that the same hands work him as worked under the late Overseer.

Ordered that Joseph Shaw be Overseer of the road from Oldhams Cabbins to the
Indian Boundary And that the hands living between said Cabbins and the Indian line
work under him.

Ordered that William Martin, Henry Tooley, and Grant Allen be commissioners
with full power to settle with the County Trustee And such settlement when made
return into this Court.

Court Adjourns until the third Monday in September next To meet at the dwelling
house of William Walton.
Test   William Walton
Sampson Williams   Peter Turney
                                              John Lancaster

At a Court Began and held at the house of William Waltons Esquire on the 20th
day of September 1802 present   Peter Turney,   Lee Sullivan
                                Arthur Hogan   John Looney
                                John Lancaster   Williams Kavanaugh
                                                       Charles Kavanaugh Esqrs.

Deed Thomas Lancaster to Jesse Powell for 363 acres proven by the oath of William Powell one of the subscribing witnesses.

James Woods Last Will and testament, was produced in Court and proven by the oath of Thomas Vance and Samuel S. Greer, subscribing witnesses. Jean Wood who was nominated Executrix of the said Will quallified accordingly and thereupon Ordered that Letters testamentary be granted to her.

Ordered that Isham Beasley be appointed Overseer of the road from Paytons Creek to Saunders ferry in the room of Henry Tooley with the hands who were under s'd Tooley.

Grand Jury :viz: James Bradley foreman Boaling Felts, Joseph, William Shaw, Philip Sutton, John Shelton William Stephenson, George Thomason, John Ward Alexander Peper, Henry Moore, Jeffrey Sutton Alexander Wilkerson, Impanneled Sworn Crarged & Sent(?) Jacob Turney Constable Sworn &C.

Deed 270 acres Samuel Shaw to James Bermingham proven by the oath of Richard Taylor one of the subscribing witnesses thereto Ordered to be registered.

William Smith Esquire produced his License as Attorney at Law. and thereupon was admitted as a practising Attorney in this Court.

Thomas Bowmans Stock mark half crop off the upper side of the right ear & an upper keel off the left.

Deed 640 Acres William McWhirter to George M McWhirter, proven by the oath of George Purtle one of the subscribing witnesses thereto ordered to be Registered.

Deed 320 acres Robert Hays to William Bratton Proven by the oath of George M. McWhirter one of the subscribing witnesses ordered to be registered.

Ordered that John Gordon be allowed Tavern License to be kept at his own house. and that he be rated according rates, who came into Court & gave Security accordingly.

P 72   Ordered that William Sullivan Senr. Robert Rowland, John Warren, Judd Strother Michael Williamson be a Jury to view mark & lay off a road leaving the Fort Blount road at the Defeated Creek hill thence a long Sullivans road to Buffelow Creek thence down said Creek to the mouth thence up Cumberland River on the South Side the nearest and best way to Waltons road and that they make report to the present Term of this Court and that William Sullivan Senr. have leave to keep a ferry on Cumberland river near the mouth of Buffelow Creek and that the Ferry kept by said Sullivan 3 miles above said Creek be discontinued.

Ordered that George Leeper, Henry Sadler, Wm. Calhoon Thomas Williamson Michael Williamson, John Kellensworth William Anderson, & Charles Carter, be a Jury to View, mark, & lay off, a road, f Squire Waltons road, directly at the head of Bartons Creek down said Creek the nearest & best way to John Williamsons ferry on Cumberland River from thence the nearest & best way to Willivan road and make report thereof to our next Court.

Ordered that all persons, who have failed to give in a list of their Taxable property in Smith County for the year 1802 make return thereof any time during the present Term.

Deed 320 Acres Pleasant Emmerson to Robert Furlong was acknowleged by said Emmerson & Ordered to be registered.

Court Adjourns until Tomorrow morning nine oclock.

Tuesday September the 21st 1302 Court met according to Adjournment, present Charles Kavanaugh,
John Lancaster
James Roberts Esquires Justices &C.

Deed 240 Acres of Land Thomas Hickman to Elijah Gaddy proven by the oath of Charles Kava naugh one of the subscribing witnesses thereto.

P 73   Deed 200 Acres of Land Henry W. Lawson to John Harvey proven by the oath of Zaddock McNew one of the subscribing witnesses thereto - Ordered to be Registered.

Deed 100 Acres Henry W. Lawson to Henkerson Rude proven by the oath of Zaddock McNew one of the subscribing witnesses thereto ordered to be Registered.

Deed 50 Acres Henry W. Lawson to Greenberry Dickson proven by the oath of Zaddock McNew one of the subscribing witnesses thereto & ordered to be registered.

Ordered that Nathaniel Brittain Esquire a Magistrate of said County Report that whereas, a warrant had issued against Zacheriah Wade and Aaron Milsted(?) under hand & seal of said Brittain for having with fource & arms cut down a Bee Tree and carried away the honey of Samuel Coruthers in Said County that Judgment the said Zachariah & Aaron and recognizance to appear at the present Term with the other proceedings thereon were in the possession of the said Nathaniel Brittain Esqr. And that said papers have been stolen lost, or mislaid - be recorded.

Ordered that Martin Young William Donoho, Reubin Goad, Tandy Witchers and Peter Dagner(?), be a Jury to view lay off and mark a road from Michael Murphys to Daniel Witchers & report to our next Court.

Ordered that Charles Kavanaugh Esquire be appointed Chairman of Smith County Court.

William Sanders Stock mark Two swallow forks Brand a cyphen S. Ordered to be recorded.

Hesekiah O'Neals Stock mark Two over half crops To be recorded &C.

Joel Holland, Josiah Howell, John Fisher, James Montgomery Lewis Casey David White, Stephen Montgomery, Joseph French are appointed a Jury to view mark & lay off a road from the County line between Smith & Sumner, to extend up said Ridge to intersect the road leading across said Ridge from Fort Blount at the most convenient place, and make report to our next Court.

Deed 175 acres Joshua Hadley to William Haynie proven by the oath of Hugh McKinnish one of the subscribing witnesses thereto Ordered to be registered.

Bill of Sail John L. Martin to Andrew Greer proven by the oath of George Matlock a subscribing witness thereto & Ordered to be recorded.

Ordered that George Thomason be Overseer of the road from the Bigg Hill to Michael Murphys and that Peter Turney Esquire furnish a list of hands.

Ordered that Abraham Piper Oversee the road from the mouth of Paytons Creek to Michael Murphys.

Daniel Alexander Stock mark Smooth crop off the left ear & slit in the right Ordered to be recorded.

Ordered that at December Term next this Court meet at the house of William Saunders at Bledsoeborough.

Court adjourns until tomorrow nine oclock.

Wednesday morning morning September 22nd 1802 Court met according to adjournment Members present (viz) Charles Kavanaugh,
                                    Nathaniel Brittain,
                                    Peter Turney,
                                    Williams Kavanaugh,
                                    James Roberts.

Ordered that Henry Dancer Oversee the road beginning at the three forks of
the road between Mingles Gap and Coruthers horse mill to extend to Richard Brittains bounds leading up middle Goose Creek.

P 75   An application of Samuel Donelson Esqr. attorney for Henry W. Lawson
ordered that the Clerk Issue a warrant directed to Charles Kavanaugh Thomas
Smith and John Lancaster Esquires commanding them to attend on the Lands of John
Kingberry in order to perpetuate Testimony relative to the boundaries of Henry
W. Lawson on the Caney fork and that publication be made in the Nashville Gazette
according to Law.

Ordered that John Luke be exonerated from the payment of his Taxes for the
year 1802 upon five black poles.

Ordered that Boling Felts oversee the Road leading from his his own house to
the Nashville road and that John Lancaster furnish a list of hands to work on
said road.

Dennis Kelly to Joseph Gordon 228 acres of land proven by the oath of John
Looney one of the subscribing witnesses Ordered to be registered.

A List of the Venire to the next County Court (viz) Godfrey Fowler, Daniel
Hammock, Edward Farris, Michael Murphy, John Payne David Cochran, James Cochran
John Brevard Jabus Gifford Abram Thompson, John Johnson, John Douglass, Philip
Day Charles McMurry, John Hargis, William Hargis, Isham Beasley, Thomas Bowman
Robert Bowman William Boyd Abram Brittain, Andrew Greer, Philip Thurman William
Payne, William Edwards, William Hankins, Samuel Coruthers, William Cord, Samuel
Hughs Bill Hughs John Murphy, John Murphy, William Alexander Daniel Alexander,
James Butler(?), Leonard Ballow and David Rorix.

A list of the Venire to the November Superior Court of Mero District Nath.
Brittain Joseph Collins Peter Turney and Edward Settles.

P 76   Ordered that William Sullivan Senr. be appointed Overseer of the road
from the Fort Blount road to Sullivans Ferry on Cumberland river near the mouth
of Buffelow Creek and that the hands on Defeated Creek below the said Road work
on the same.

William Richards & Moses Ashbrooks and all the other hands above said road,
who live nearer to it than the Fort Blount Road.

Ordered that Robert Rowland oversee the road from Waltons road to Sullivans
Ferry and that the hands on Indian Creek and Harricane Creek and in Sullivans
Bent(Bend?) work on the same.

Report of the Jury relative to the road from Defeated Creek Hill near
fourt Blount road.

We the Jurors appointed by the Court of Smith County on Monday 20th September 1802 to lay off a road beginning at Defeated Creek Hill on the Fourt
Blount road crossing Cumberland river near the mouth of Buffeloe Creek and to
intersect Walton road at the head of Snow Creek have laid off and marked the

same according to Law.

Report of Jury &c. We the Jurors of a road from Charles Kavanaughs to intersect the road leading from William Waltons at or near John Campbells on said road have laid off and marked the same agreeable to the appointement of the Court at last Term.

Ordered that Isaac Moore be appointed Overseer of the said road from the house of Charles Kavanaugh Esq. to the Flat rock branch on Hickmans Creek, and that all the hands living North of said branch including the hands on the waters of Hickmans Creek, between it & Bishops road above said branch work on the same.

P 77   Ordered also that Zadock McNew be appointed Overseer of the above road from the mouth of the flat rock branch to a Ford on the Caney fork near the house of Thomas Esquire and all the hands on the Waters of Hickmans Creek below the mouth of said branch work on said road excepting the hands of Thomas Smith Esquire Enos Herell & the two Pierces.

Ordered also that John Gordon Esqr. be appointed Overseer of the above road from the above mentioned ford over the Caney fork to its intersection with Waltons road and that the hands living in the Snow Creek Settlement together with the hands excepted above work on the same.

Ordered that Willis Jones be appointed Overseer of the road leading from Richard Banks ferry to the house of Williams Kavanaugh Esquire as far as to its intersection with the road leading from Waltons road to the Bigg Spring, and that all the hands on the East side of said road to Cumberland river to include the hands of Richard Banks work on the same.

Ordered that Court adjourn until Court in Course.

Charles Kavanaugh Chairman

At a Court opened and held for the County of Smith on Monday the 20th day of December 1802. Members present (viz) Peter Turney,
James Hibits ,and
Williams Kavanaugh Esqrs.

Thomas Wright came into Court and resigned his appointment as constable.

Ordered that Daniel Alexander be appointed Constable who came into Court gave security & quallified according to Law.

William L. Alexander exhibited his stock mark being two swallow forks and an under keel in the right ordered to be recorded.

William Martin came into Court, and resigned his appointment as overseer of the roads, and Godfrey Fowler is appointed in his place the same hands to work under him as were liable to work under the late Overseer.

P 78   Ordered that the report of the Jury who were appointed to view and mark the road from Michael Murphys to Daniel Witchers be received which is the way said Witcher moved his family.

Grand Jury (towit), Leonard Ballow, Abraham Brittain, Isham Beasley, Thomas Bowman, David Rorax William Alexander, Daniel Hammock, Godfrey Fowler, Philip Day, Charles McMurry, David Cochran, and Williams Hankins, who being Elected & sworn received their charge and sent out, and Jacob Turney is appointed Constable to attend them.

Deed 640 Acres James Easten to Joseph Cruckshanks(?) proven by the oath of Thomas Dillon one of the subscribing witnesses thereto.

Deed 191 acres William Saunders to James McClain Acknowleged.

Deed 800 acres William Saunders to Alexander Lowry Acknowleged.

John Caplinger came into Court and resigned his appointment as Overseer of the road & John Tuggle is appointed in his stead, with the same hands to work under him & &C.

Ordered that John Caplinger be allowed to build a mill on Round Lick Creek on the land belonging to himself & Harris Bradford & that he be allowed the customary rates of toll for grinding.

Court adjourns until tomorrow 10 oclock

Tuesday the 21st Courts met according to adjournment Members present (viz)
James Hibits,
Peter Turney,
Elmore Douglass
John Lancaster and
James Draper Esquires Justices.

Ordered that the inventory account of the Estate of James Wood, deceasd., returned into Court be received.

Ordered that the fine & cost incurred by Willie Sullivan for his not attending as a Juror at this Court to March Term last to be remitted.

Letter of Attorney, William Brice Fontvielle(?) to Lee Sullivan was proven by the oath of Abraham Rogers a subscribing Witness.

Ordered that Rhoda Powell have letters of Administration on the Estate of Jessee Powell Deceased who came into Court gave Security & quallified according to Law.

P 79   Deed 280 Acres Joseph Laurence to John Warren proven by the oath of Lee Sullivan a subscribing witness thereto ordered to be registered.

Letter of Attorney Wilson Cage to Lewis Davis Acknowleged in open Court.

Deed 130 Acres John Murphy to Samuel Hughs Proven by the oath of Richard Brittain one of the subscribing witnesses.

Deed 10 acres Henry W. Lawson to Barnibas Powell proven by the oath of Silas Jernigan one of the subscribing witnesses thereto Ordered to be Registered.

Deed 125 acres John Croslin to Freeman Burrow proven by the oath of James Hibits one of the subscribing witnesses ordered to be registered.

James Cherry Exhibited his Stock mark being a crop of each ear and an under keel in the right Ordered to be recorded.

Ordered that Lee Sullivan Esqr. be Overseer of the road from Willivans to Sullivans Ferry and that the hands liable to work on said below Hurricane Creek work under said Overseer.

Ordered that Charles I. Love be allowed to a list of his taxable property for the year 1802 who returned the same & paid the tax to the Sheriff.

Ordered that Judd Strother & John Gordon be valuers of property under execution in Captains Sullivans Company and that Thomas Draper & Willeroy Pate be valuers of property under Execution in in Captain Pates Company William Marchbanks and George Leeper in Capt. Andersons Company.

Court Adjourns until Tomorrow nine oclock.

Wednesday December the 22nd Court met according to adjournment Members present
(Towit) James Hibits,
      Lee Sullivan,
      John Looney,
      James Draper,
      James Gwin and
      Williams Kavanaugh Esquires Justices.

John Chambers Exhibited his Stock mark being a crop off the right ear & a
Slit in each Ordered to be Recorded.

P 80   Jesse Beasley Exhibited his Stock mark being a Swallow fork in the left
ear and an under keel in the right Ordered that the same be recorded.

James Gwin Esqr. Exhibited his Stock mark being a crop & slit in the left
and an over slope in the right Ordered to be recorded.

In the suit Nathaniel Ridley against Reuben Osburn James Draper and Jesse
Shoemake came into Court and replevied the property attachd. and acknowleged
themselves as special Bail.

Ordered that the following Justices, take in the list of taxable property
for the year 1803, viz. James Gwin for Captain Caseys Company James Draper for
Captain Witchers Company, James Hibits for Captain Giffords Company John Patterson
for Cap Pattersons Company, Tilman Dixon for Cap Matlocks Company William Gregory
for Cap Settles Company James Roberts for Cap Pates Company and Cap Andersons
Company Lee Sullivan for Cap Sullivans Company John Lancasters for Cap Fights
Company John Loancy(?) for Cap Hays Company Charles Kavanaugh for Cap Kavanaughs
Company, William Kavanaugh for Cap. Cottons Company Elmore Douglass for Captain
Bishops Company Peter Turney for Cap Samuels Company.

Godfrey Shaver Exhibited his Stock mark, in open Court being two slits in
the right ear & a crop off the left Ordered to be recorded.

Ordered that Mathew Green be fined the sum of thirty-one & a fourth cents
for profanely swearing in Court, and that Execution Issue against him for the
aforesaid sum.

Deed 50 acres John Sedgley To Henry Dancer, proven by the oath of Daniel
Burford a subscribing witness thereto Ordered to be Registered.

Bill of Sail Jonas Dancer Senr. to Dancer Junr. proven by the oath of
Daniel Burford one of the subscribing witnesses thereto and ordered to be recorded.

Bill of Sail Jonas Dancer, to Thomas Shoate and Manuel Hunter proven by the
oath of Daniel Burford a subscribing witness thereto.

P 81   Deed of Gift James Dancer to Henry Dancer to children proven by the oath
of Daniel Burford one of the subscribing witnesses.

Ordered that the following hands work under Daniel Alexander Overseer of the
road (viz) Elisha Oglesby, James Oglesby, Hugh Stephenson, Josiah Howell, Joel
Holland, John Kenedy, Joseph Sullivan, Owen Sullivan, Isaac Sullivan, Thomas
Larimore, Thomas Wimbs, John Nichol, Richd. Barver (Bowen?), Peter Startuck.

Deed 100 Acres Henry W. Lawson to John Shaver proven by the oath of Godfrey

Shaver one of the subscribing witnesses Let it be Registered.

Deed 150 Acres Dan Williams to Andrew Johnson Kavanaugh proven by the oath of James Scoby & John Baker two subscribing witnesses Let it be registered.

Court adjourns until Tomorrow nine oclock.

Tuesday December 23rd 1802 Court met according to adjournment (Members present) [to wit) James Gwin,
Elmore Douglass
James Draper and
Nathaniel Brittain Esquires.

The last Will & Testament of John Payne Deceased was Exhibited in open Court, the execution whereof Peter Turney Esquire proved by his oath, who also swore that he saw Thomas Farris subscribe the same with himself as a witness also a memorandum on note on the back of said Will Peter Hudspeth the subscribing came into Court and proved the Execution thereof and the said Peter Turney and Emd. Farris quallified as Executors aforesaid.

Ordered that Reubin Hall be bound to Joel Dyer untill he arrive to the age of twenty one years he being now about six years old, and the said Joel Dyer came into Court and entered into an Indenture with the chairman of the Court and also P 82   Court and also agreed to learn, him the said Reubin Hall the Blacksmiths, and to have him learned, to read, write & cypher as far as the Rule of three & give him a Set of Black Smith tools when he becomes free.

Ordered that Vallentine Billiff to be bound to Andrew Greer until he arrive at age of twenty one years he now being about Sixteen years of age & the said Andrew Greer came into Court and entered into an Indenture with the Chairman of the said Vallentine Balliff with sixty six dollars and two thirds & a good saddle & Bridle and freedom Cloaths and a good English Education.

Ordered that Margarett Hall be bound to Isaac Johns until She arrive at the age of Eighteen years being now about nine years of age and the said Johns Came into Court and entered into Indenture with the Chearman of the Court of Smith County.

Ordered that John Jenkins be Overseer of that part of the road where Henry Huddleston was late Overseer and that the same hands work under him as were liable to work under the late Overseer with the addition of Francis Caps & William Richards.

Ordered that the report of the Jury who viewed & marked the Road from the line between Smith & Sumner Counties & on the Ridge between Goose Creek & Barren Waters to Tandy Witchers be received and that Stephen Montgomery be Overseer to open & keep the same in repair & that all the hands living on said Ridge below where the Fort Blount road crosses the ridge work under sd. Overseer.

Ordered that William Marchbanks & William Caldhoon each be Overseer to open & keep a road as laid out & marked by a Jury down Martons Creek to Williamsons ferry & from thence till it intersects Sullivans road & the hands on the waters of Martons creek work under them.

P 83   Court adjourns until tomorrow nine oclock.

Friday December the 24th 1802 Court met according to Adjournment Members (viz) James Hibits,
Elmore Douglass &
Williams Kavanaugh Esquires Justices.

Ordered that William L. Alexander, Isham Beasley and Anthony Samuel, be Patroers (Partners?) in Captain Samuel Company.

Ordered that Charles I. Love be fined the sum of five dollars for his non-attendance as a Juror, at the present term and that Execution Issue against him immediately for the aforesaid sum fine remitted.

Ordered that William Haglan be Overseer of the road from Snow Creek on the Caney fork road to Charles Kavanaughs and that Zachariah Ford, Mr. Thurmans, & Mr. Shoemakes hands work under said Overseer.

Veni. Fa. to the ensuing County Court, vizt, Benjamin Clark, Soloman Harpole, Hesekiah Woodard, Robert Dugan, Edward James, David Looney, Jeremiah Taylor, Richard Brittain, Job Bass, James Hunter, Robert Ward, James W. Wright, Harriss Bradford, Andrew Greer, William Martin, Vincent Ridley, William Douglass, Phillip Sitton, Elisha Oglesby, George McWhirter, Benjamin Barton, Henry Tooley, Fredrick Turner, John Barkley, William Penny, John Rankers (Rankins?), James Gibson, Micurm(?) Henry, Isham Beasley, William Stalcup, Grant Allen, Jeffrey Sitton, John Johnson of E. Goose Creek, John Rutherford, Francis Patterson, and Wilson Cage.

Ordered that Mathew Payne, Enos Harrold, William Lancaster, Thomas Smith, John Reece, Robert Smith, and Mathew Harper, be appointed Jurors of view, to lay off a road from the mouth of Caney Fork to Lancasters mill and make report to o`` next Court.

A Deed 70 Acres Samuel Shaw to Thomas Smith proven by the oath of James Birmingham one of the subscribing witnesses.

Ordered that John Gordon and Benjamin Holland, be appraisers to appraise the Estate of James Wood Deceased and to return the same into our ensuing County Court.

P 84   Ordered that William Walton have letters of Administration on the Estate of Elizabeth Hall Deceased, who came into Court gave Security & quallified according to Law.

William Hargis, Exhibitted his stock mark in open Court, being two smoth crops & a slit in the right ear, Ordered to be recorded.

Ordered that William Martin, Edward Settles and Thomas Draper, be commissioners to divide the lands of William Young Deceased between the heirs and also to lay off one third to the widow of said Deceased.

John Brevard exhibited his Stock mark smooth crop off the left ear, & half crop in the right, under side.

Ordered that Moses Hart be allowed the sum of one dollar pr. day for taking care of Griffin West a pauper from this time until it shall appear from the testimony of Doctor Wilson Yandle(?) the attending Physician that a less sum will be sufficient for his maintenance and the necessary attendances, and from that time such sum as the Court shall hereafter Judge to be sufficient.

Ordered that the following report of the Sheriff for Taxable property not returned for Taxation for the year 1802 be received John Smith, 1280 acres Round Lick Creek Peter Black 640 Ditto- Robert Williamson, 274 acres Mulherins Creek David Shelton 960 acres on Round lick Creek, Daniel Anderson 640 Mulherins Creek Colo. Gideon Lamb. 5000 acres Round Lick Creek, John Ford 1560 Round lick Creek Samuel love 1508 Round lick Creek, Robert King 640 Joining the South & East boundaries of 1000 acres known by the name of Harts land - Joshua Hadley 640 acres Round Lick Creek - William Hay 2560 Clendinins(?) Creek - Francis Childs 3840 acres Caney Fork - William Fereby 3060 - John Allen 3560 Caney Fork - Stephen Lyn 100 acres - Thomas Capbell 274 - Robert Douglass 2560 - Archibald Felts 1000 acres - John Law, 640 acres - Baker Archer 640 acres William Russell 640 acres - Jacob Adams 640 acres Robert Reddin 640 acres Redmond D. Barry 428 acres Salt lick Creek, P 85   Redmond D. Barry 428 acres Salt lick Creek, Redmond D. Barry 640 acres

Martin Creek Do 640 acres Martins Creek Do 640 acres Indian Creek - the same 1000 acres South Side of Cumberland John Hall 2560 acres South Side Cumberland.

Ordered that a copy of the aforesaid land reported be forth with Transmitted to the Printer of the Knoxville Gazette and that he be directed to publish the same twice in the Knoxville & Tennessee Gazettes.

Ordered that Dyer Ford, Andrew Greers hands Mr. Turnbulls hands, William Short, McCearley (or Mr. Cearly), John Barr. and George Kirkland work under John Johnson Hatter, in addition to his other hands. And such other hands as Nathaniel Brittain shall furnish said Overseer within his bounds.

Court Adjourns until Court in Course to meet at this place.

Nathaniel Brittain

Test
Sampson Williams

Elmore Douglass
Tilman Dixon

At a Court opened & held for the County of Smith on Monday the 21st March 1803, Members present (vizt) Elmore Douglass
Lee Sullivan &
Tilman Dixon Esquires.

Deed 220 Acres William Sullivan to George Leeper, proven by the oath of Lee Sullivan one of the Subscribing Witnesses.

Deed 240 acres Henry King to Moses James proven by the oath of John Lovelady one ofthe subscribing witnesses.

Deed 1380 Acres Samuel Parker to John Billingsley proven by the oath of Sampson Williams a subscribing witness thereto.

Deed 100 acres Joseph Collins to Solomon Thomas proven by the oath of Thomas Allen a subscribing witness thereto and Ordered to be Registered.

P 86   Then the venire facias returned by the Sheriff, the following persons were Elected to serve as Grand Jurors the present Term, vizt. William Staloup, Benjamin Barton, Elisha Oglesby, Hesekiah Woodard, Isham Beasley, Harris Bradford, John Rutherford, Frederick Tarver(?) James Gibson, John Barclay Henry Tooley, foreman David Looney and James Hunter. Daniel Alexander was sworn as Constable to attend them.

Deed 169½ acres Joseph Collins to Thomas Allen proven by the oath of James Ketchring(?) a subscribing witness thereto Ordered to be registed.

Deed 41.3/4 acres Maj. John Young to Jacob Kenedy Proved by the oath of Lee Sullivan a subscribing witness thereto.

Deed 220 acres Joshua Knowlton to William Kelton Proved by the oath of Stephen Montgomery & George Anderson, subscribing witnesses thereto.

Deed 320 acres Henry Gamble to Booker Bradford Proved by the oath of Joseph Pait, a subscribing witness thereto. Ordered to be registered.

Deed 640 acres Joseph Fan (or Fox?) to Joseph Gifford Proved by the oath of Jabez Gifford a subscribing witness Ordered to be registered.

Deed 130 acres John L. Martin to Willis P. Ellis acknowleged and Ordered to be registered.

William Stephenson Exhibited his stock mark in open Court being a crop off the left ear Ordered to be recorded.

John Lovin Maxy Exhibited his stock mark being a crop & slit in the right ear
& a swallow fork in the left, ordered to be recorded.

William Stalcup Exhibited his stock mark being a slit & under bit in the right
ear Ordered to be recorded.

Solomon Harpole Exhibited his stock mark in open Court being a smooth crop
off the left ear & an under bit out of the right Ordered to be recorded.

Samuel Donelson heretofore County Solicitor came into Court & resigned said
appointment & William Smith Esquire Attorney at law is appointed in his stead, who
P 87   als came into Court & took the necessary oaths.

Ordered that Martin Young be Overseer to open & keep in repair the road as
layed off from Daniel Witchers to Aaron Lawses and that the hands adjacent thereto
work under said Overseer.

Ordered that Lewis Pipkin, be overseer to open & keep in repair that part of
the road as laid off by a Jury from Daniel Witchers to the State line near Peter
Kings said Overseer to begin at Aaron Laws & work to the State line and that all
the hands adjacent thereto work under him.

Ordered that Thomas Draper be Overseer of the road from Pleasant Kearbys to
Tandy Witchers and that all the hands living on the East fork of Salt Lick Creek
& Wartrace Creek work under him.

Ordered that the late the late order of Court for viewing and marking a road
from the County line near the Wartrace Creek to cross Cumberland River at the mouth
of said Creek & up said Creek till it intersects the road leading from Fort Blount
to Witchers at the most convenient place be received.

Jarrol Wright Exhibited his Stock mark being a crop off the right ear & a
half penny in the upper side of the same & a half penny in the under side of the
left Ordered to be recorded.

Richard Taylor Overseer of the road &C. resigns his commission and James
Bermingham appointed in his stead.

Ordered that the Court Adjourn till Tomorrow nine oclock.

Tuesday morning March 22nd 1803. The Court met according to adjournment
Members present (vizt) Elmore Douglass,
                 James Hibits, and
                 James Draper Esquires Justices &C.

Deed 113 acres John Croslin to Edward James proved by the oath of James Hibits
a subscribing witness thereto.

Deed of Gift Edward Bromfield, to John Bromfield Tharon Bromfield, Elizabeth
Bromfield, Mary Bromfield Proven by the oath of John Dickson a subscribing witness
ordered to be recorded.

P 88   Daniel Alexander Overseer resigned & William L. Alexander is appointed in
his stead with the same hands to work under him that formerly worked under Daniel
Alexander.

Ordered that John Lovelady & Andrew Jones have letters of Administration on
the Estates of Moses Jones Junr. and Moses Jones Senr. who came into Court gave
Security and quallified according to Law. and also returned into Court an Inventory
of the aforesaid Estates.

Deed 156 acres, James Mulherin to Henry Tooley, Proved by the oath of Elisha Oglesby a subscribing witness thereto.

Deed Thomas Masten Collector of Direct Tax for 8th collection District in the State of Tennessee to William P. Anderson for 640 acres Proved by the oath of George Smith & Henry Bradford Subscribing witnesses thereto.

Deed 1000 acres Thomas Masten collector of Direct Tax &C. to William P. Anderson & Henry Bradford Proved by the oath of George Smith a subscribing witness thereto.

Deed 640 acres Thomas Masten collector of Direct Tax &C. To Henry Bradford Proved by the oath of George Smith a subscribing witness thereto ordered to be registered.

Ordered that Landy Shoemake & John Jenkins each be allowed Tavern Licence to keep an ordinary at there now dwelling house & that they be rated agreeable to the costomary rates in this County of Retailors who came into Court and gave Security accordingly.

Daniel Draper came into Court and resigned his appointment as constable.

Harvey Johns is appointed a Constable for this county who gave bond with Benjamin Johns & Willis Jones his Securities and took the oaths prescribed by law.

The Grand Jury returned into Court & returned a bill of Indictment against
P 89   Mathew Green "a true Bill" and withdrew to consider further presentments.

Ordered that Moses Hart be allowed the sum of sixteen dollars for attending on a certain Greffin West, and that Amos Freeman be allowed the Sum of Eleven Dollars for taking care of said West eleven days to be paid out of any County monies not otherwise appropriated.

Josiah Payne came into Court and resigned his appointment as Overseer of the Road and Jese Johnson is appointed in his stead the same hands to work under him as were liable to work under the late Overseer.

Ordered that John Williamson be allowed to keep a Ferry at the mouth of Martins Creek and that he be allowed to receive the costomary rates for ferrying &C. who came into Court & gave security according to Law.

William Sullivan Senior who heretofore obtained an order for a ferry at the mouth of Buffeloe Creek came into Court & gave bond and security according to Law and was rated as above.

An Inventory account of the Estate of John Payne Deceased returned into Court by Peter Turney one of the Executors ordered to be recorded.

Deed 270 acres William Saunders to Garrett Wright acknowleged.

Ordered that Mathew Harper be allowed to build a Grist Mill on Hickmans Creek on his own land and that he be allowed the costomary rates of toll for grinding.

Deposition of John Hallum sworn to in open Court ordered to be Recorded.

Deed 119 acres of Land John Barkley to William Penny acknowleged in open Court, Ordered to be Registered.

Ordered that Abram Gregory be appointed Constable who came into Court gave Security & quallified according to Law.

Ordered that Thomas R. Short be appointed Constable who came into Court gave Security & quallified according to Law.

P 90   Ordered that Harvey Johns be appointed Constable who came into Court gave security and quallified according to Law.

Court adjourns until Tomorrow nine oclock.

Wednesday March the 23d 1803 Court met according to adjournment members present (vizt) Tilman Dixon,
                Elmore Douglass
                John Lancaster,
                Peter Turney &
                James Hibits Esquires Justices.

Ordered that the Petition of the heirs & Devesees of Thomas Parsons Decd. Exhibited to this Court by Redmond D. Barry Esquire their attorney to take the Deposition of Robert Thompson, & Charles Green in order to Establish the boundaries & other Specialties called for in said Grant being a Tract commonly called Dingsberries Tract be filed of record and that their Testimony be perpetuated according to Law.

Ordered that the resignation of Basil Shaw Oversser of the road be received, and that James Walker be appointed in his stead and that the same hands that were liable to work under the late overseer work under him.

Ordered that James Roberts, Sampson Williams, Edward Jinnings, and John Lancaster be Jurors for the Superior Court.

Ordered that William Payne be appointed Overseer of the road in the room of Silas Rolls, who has this day resigned and that the same hands work under him as was liable to work under the late Overseer.

Ordered that the resignation of Zedekiah Ingram as Constable be received.

Ordered that Mathew Payne Overseer of the Road from Waltons ferry to Mulherins Creek, and that Thomas Smith Esqr. give said Overseer a list of hands.

Ordered that Enos Harrold be Overseer to keep in repair a road as laid out by a Jury from Mulherins Creek to Bolings branch and that Thomas Smith Esqr. furnishd. Overseer with a list of hands.

P 91   Ordered that William Lancaster be Overseer to open & keep in repair a Road from Bolings branch to Lancasters road and that Thomas Smith Esquire furnish said Overseer with a list of hands.

The Grand Jury returned into Court & presented Buchanan Russell Andrew Mitcalf(?) William Rollen and Samuel Avits as guilty of profane swearing in the verge of the Court, and withdrew to consider of further presentments.

Ordered that the following persons be appointed to serve as Jurors at the ensuing term of this Court and that a writ of Venire facias Issue accordingly (viz) Michael Murphy, John Sloan, Edward Suttles, Abraham Piper, Solomon Blair, John Piper, John Davis, Samuel Staloup, Isaac Johns, Elijah Raney, Edmond Jinnings John Morris, Samuel Evetts, John Cochran, James Cochran, John Sitton, Philip Sitton, William Sitton Thomas Sitton, Francis Pattersons, Basil Shaw, James Smith, George McWhirter, Abraham Thompson, Rece(?) Hughs, Samuel Hughs, John Sedgley, Hugh Stephenson Junr. Robert McNeeley, Francis Finley, Alexander Kenedy.

Ordered that Samuel Staloup be appointed guardian of Ame Clark Andrew Clark, and James Clark, orphan children who thereupon give bond in the sum of three hundred dollars with William Saunders & Andrew Greer his securities according to Law.

Ordered that the Grand Jury be discharged.

Ordered that Grant Allen, John Shelton William Stalcup, James Gibson, Samuel Coruthers be a Jury to view lay off and mark, a road from Banks ferry, to the forks of the road, near Coruthers Still House.

Ordered that Stephen Farmer, George Noggle, John Caplinger, Samuel Caplinger be taken from John Tuggles hands, as Overseer of the Road and added to James Wrathers hands as Overseer afsd.

P 92   Ordered that there be a County tax of 6¼ cents laid on each 100 acres of land and 6¼ cents laid on each 100 acres of land and 6¼ on each white Pole & 6¼ cents on each Black Poll, and 25 cents on each Stud Horse.

Ordered that Jacob Kenedy be allowed to build a Grist Mill on his own Land, on Defeated Creek and that he be allowed the costomary rates of Toll for Grinding.

Ordered that all the hands between the Bledsowborough road and Cumberland River, work from Bishops Ferry to Nathaniel Merritts and that Jacob Caplinger be Overseer, and that the ballance of the hands who were liable to work under John Scoby from Nathaniel Merith, to the cross Roads, leading from the Round Lick to the Big Springs.

Ordered that Thomas Draper, Willeroy Pate and Nathaniel Ridley be patrolls in Cap Pates Company.

Bond for 100 dollars John Young to Jacob Kenedy proven by the Oath of Lee Sullivan one of the subscribing Witnesses.

Anthony Samuel Exhibited his stock mark in open Court being a crop & slit in the right ear and an under bit out of the bottom of the left ear Ordered to be recorded.

Ordered that Court adjourn until Court in course to meet at the dwelling house of Tilman Dixon.   Peter Turney
Test   Thomas Smith
Sampson Williams   John Lancaster

At a Court opened & held at Dixons Springs at the House of Tilman Dixon on Monday the 20th day of June 1803, Members present   (vizt) Tilman Dixon,
                                                     Elmore Douglass,
                                                     Charles Kavanaugh,
                                                     Peter Turney, and
                                                     John Lancaster Esquires
                                                                    Justices.

P 93   The following persons were drawn from the Venire returned to this Term as Grand Jurors, vizt, Bazzel Shaw foreman Samuel Stalcup, Michael Murphy, Solomon Blair, John Piper, John Davis, John Sloan, Abraham Thompson, Francis Patterson, Edmond Jennings, Essac Johns, Samuel Evetts, Elijah Hainey, Philip Sitton, Edward Settles who were impaneld Sworn & Charged &C. Daniel Alexander a Constable sworn to attend the foregoing Jury.

Moses Lawsons Stock mark a smooth crop of the left ear and under bit out of each ear. Ordered to be Recorded.

Huchings G. Burton Esquire produced his Licence as Attorney at Law, in this

State & thereupon is admitted to practice in this Court.

S
Deed 540 acres Richard Harmon to James Ray proved by the oath of James Ray Senr. a subscribing witness thereto Ordered to be Registered.

Deed Joshua Hadley to Abram Piper 170 acres Proven by the oath of Alexander Piper a subscribing Witness thereto.

William Pryor to John Venteos Deed for 220 acres Proved by the oath of Charles Kavanaugh a subscribing witness thereto.

The Grand Jury returned into Court and returned a Bill of Indictment against Robert Smith Slaughter "a true bill," and withdrawn to consider of Further presentment

Magness McDonald, Exhibited his Stock mark in open Court bein an upper keel in each ear Ordered to be Recorded.

Ordered that Hesekiah Woodard be Overseer of the Road from Nathaniel Merritts to the cross roads leading from the Round Lick to the big Spring on Cedar Creek and all the hands from Jacob Dices to the Wilson County line work under Said Overseer.

P 94   Deed of Gift 267 acres John Murphy Senr. to James Murphy, John Murphy Junr. Robert Barkley Murphy William Cathey, Murphy & Richard Murphy, Acknowleged in open Court and ordered to be Registered.

Court Adjourns until Tomorrow nine oclock.
                                        Sampson Williams Clk.

Tuesday June 21st Court met according to adjounment members present (vizt)
Charles Kavanaugh,
Nathaniel Brittain,
Williams Kavanaugh,
Elmore Douglass and
John Lancaster Esquires Justices &C.

Ordered that the resignation of Archibald Sloan Overseer of the road be received and that Michael Murphy be appointed in his stead, with the same hands the former Overseer had &C.

Ordered that Henry Wakefield be Overseer to open & keep in repair a road as layed out by a Jury from Daniel Witchers to Aarons Laws and that from Reuben Goads by Robert Collins & James Jones's to Martin Youngs and that all the hands adjacent thereto work under him.

Deed Arthur Hogan to William Wooton Proved by the oath of William Lane one of the subscribing Witnesses thereto.

Deed 50 Acres John Hargis to Adam Stafford acknowleged by John Hargis in proper person.

William Lock vs Joseph Russell, in this case Buckner Russell and Thomas Etchison, special bail for the Deft. surrendered him up in open Court, in discharge of themselves, therefore it is considered by the Court that they be discharged from their under taking in this behalf made.

Upon petition of Alsey Pierce, it is ordered that Samuel Stalcup pay her the sum of twenty five Dollars towards the maintenance of a bastard of the said Alseys to whom the said Samuel is reputed Father.

John Gordon Junr. Records his Stock mark, vizt, An under bit in each ear.

Deed 180¼ acres William Fate to Nicholass Seal proven by the oath of Sampson Williams one of the subscribing Witnesses thereto.

Peter Turney Esquire one of the Bail for Mathew Green on an indictment came into Court & surrendered the body of the said Green in discharge of himself & also in discharge of Aolo William Saunders the other security, who are accordingly discharged and the said Deft is thereupon ordered into the custody of the Sheriff.

Deed 246 Acres William Wooten to Benjamin proven by the oath of William Lane one of the subscribing witnesses.

Deed 20¼ acres Robert Thompson to Samuel King proved by the oath of Samuel King a subscribing witness.

Deed 61 acres Joel Holland to Josiah Howell proven by the oath of John Fisher a subscribing witness thereto.

Deed 200 Acres William Payne to George Rowling Acknowleged in open Court.

Deed Josiah Payne to William Payne 1096 Acres proven by the oath of Moses Allen one of the subscribing witnesses thereto.

The Grand Jury returned into Court & returned a presentment against Elitha Smith of having been delivered of a Base begotten Child the Father of which shh has yet made known in manner prescribed by law. Also a presentment against Levi Casey & Josiah Payne for an Effray and withdrew to consider of further Presentments & Indictments.

Court Adjourns until Tomorrow Eight Oclock Wednesday June the 23r 1803.

Court met according to Adjournment Members present, vizt.
William Walton
Peter Turney
James Hibbits
John Patterson
John Lancaster
Thomas Smith and
John Looney Esquires Justices.

P 96   Deed 320 acres James Robertson to William Smith Proved by the oath of Thomas Stuart a subscribing witness.

Deed 100 Acres Isaac Morgan to James Jinkins Proven by the oath of Thomas Smith one of the subscribing witnesses thereto.

The Grand Jury returned into Court & Exhibited a bill of Indictment against Leonard Fite & withdrew to consider of other Indictments.

Ordered that the account & settlement of James Given Esquire Treasurer of Smith County as stated by Henry Tooley Grant Allen, and William Martin be filed of record and that the said James Givin have a credit of five hundred & thirty six dollars forty four cents.

Ordered that Joel Dyer be appointed Guardian for his Sister Betsey she having mad choice of him & was approved of by Court who came into Court & gave Security accordingly.

Ordered that Jarrot Wright be allowed to build a Grist mill upon his own Land upon Line Creek and that he be allowed the costomary rates of Toll for grinding.

Bill of Sail Lazarus Cotten to James Hart proven by the oath of Charles

Burton a subscribing witness thereto.

The Grand Jury returned into Court and Exhibited three presentments, Vizt, one against Nancy Taylor for having been delivered of a base born child, the Father of which she has not yet made known, Also a presentment, against Charles C Cotten a Pedler for profanity swearing als one against Andrew Hamilton for profanily swearing repeatedly.

Ordered that John Fisher, William Bartlet, William Henderson and John Cooper be discharged from all fines imposed upon them in consequence of their non attendance as witnesses on Bail in behalf of the State against a certain Dempsey P 97 Kenedy, or in consequence of a certain Scire Facias or Scire Facias's Issued against them from December Term, last, returnable to March Term last.

The Grand Jury returned into Court & Exhibited a presentment Against Andrew Hamilton for profanely swearing & withdrew to consider of further presentments.

Ordered that Henry Tooley, Grant Allen & William Martin commissioners appointed to Settle with the County Trustee be allowed in manner prescribed by Law for two days services and that a copy of this order be a sufficient voucher to the Treasurer or Trustee to pay them.

The grand Jury returned into Court & Exhibitted a presentment against James Black (a Blacksmith) for profanely and Blasphemenously repeatedly calling upon the name of his Maker, and then withdrew to consider of further presentments.

Court Adjourns until Tomorrow eight oclock.

Tuesday June 23d Court met according to adjournment members present, vizt,
James Givin
James Hibits
Peter Turney
Charles Kavanaugh, and
John Looney Esquires.

Ordered that John Lancaster, William Lancaster, and William Powell, be commissioners to take the Deposition of Robert Thompson Charles Green & others of them to be taken on the premises of a tract of Land commonly called Kingberrys Tract and at a Springson called Kingsberrys Spring on Hickmans Creek in Smith County in the Stateof Tennessee, in order to establish said Spring and other Specialties called for in the Grant and Location to be taken on the first day of September next in order to perpetuate their testimony agreeable to an act of Assembly in such case made & provided. This testimony to be taken & perpetuated for and in behalf of the Heirs & Devesees of Thomas Parsons Deceasd.

P 98 The Grand Jury returned into Court & Exhibited a Bill of Incictment against Anthony Hogan"a true bill," And the Court being informed by the County Solicitor, there was no other business, to be brought before the Grand Jury, ordered that they be discharged from further attendance.

The following persons were appointed to serve as Jurors at the next County Court (vizt). John Gray, Edmond Boaz, David Rorix, Nicholas Shrum, Jacob Burriss, Daniel Hammock, Jacob Harvick, Philip Day, William Douglass, Charles McMurry, Thomas Armstrong, James W. Wright, James Smith, David Keighlough, Stephen Jones, Moses Hurt, David Laurence, Jaby Gifford Joseph Gifford, David Jennings, Joel Holland, Stephen Montgomery, Leonard Ballow, Elias Johns, Isham Beasley Edward Farris, Moses Allen, Larkin Bethel, Patrick Donoho, Charles Forrester, John Gordon Mathew Payne, Zaddock McNew, William Hughes, John Fite Senkor, Lewis Ford Stephen Robertson Senr. Bowling Felts, Zedekiah Ingram, William Wooten, William Lane, George Roland and Stephen Anderson,

Deed 4800 acres Joseph Westbrook & wife to Henry W. Lawson Proven by the oath of Armistead Stubblefield one of the subscribing witnesses.

Deed 108 acres Arthur Hogan to John Vines, Acknowleged in open Court.

Ordered that Sampson Williams Clerk of Smith County be allowed the sum sixty Dollars for his ex officio Services, from the time of his acting as clerk, until the third Monday of December last.

Ordered that John Douglass Sheriff and Collector be allowed the sum of
P 99   Eighty Dollars for his ex officio Services from the first of March 1802 to the first of March 1803.

Ordered that William Smith Esquire Solicitor of Smith County be allowed ten dollars for his fees, on four Scire facias's in the case of the State against Cannady.

Ordered that Henry Bohannan be overseer of that part of Caney Fork Road from the head of Snow Creek to William Kellys and that all hands who were liable to work under William Pryor the late Overseer work under him.

Ordered that Enos Harrold Overseer of the road from Mulherins Creek to Bolings branch, continue to a certain large Spring on said branch.

Ordered that William Lancaster Overseer of the road from Lancaster Road to Bolings branch continue down said branch to a certain large Spring so as to meet the road opened by Enos Harrold. Also that the Shumakes who heretofore were liable to work under Enos Harrold hereafter work under Mathew Payne.

Ordered that Thomas Draper, Sampson Williams, Henry Huddleston, Peter Turney, Joel Dyer, Junr. George Thomason and Edward Settles be a jury to view & make such alterations as they may think necessary, form Thomas Jinkins at the foot of Defeated Creek Hill to Edward Farrises and report the same to our next Court.

Ordered that a Jury be appointed to view & lay off & Mark a road from Esquire Kavanaughs to intersect Bumpass road at the County line and that the following persons be a Jury, to wit, John Vantrice, Elijah Gaddy, George Tinkle, Thomas Flood, John Moore, Isaac Conger, Charles Kavanaugh and Benjamin Kavanaugh
P 100   to view the same.

Ordered that Berryman Turner be Overseer of the Road from where Willis Jones quits working to where it intersects the road leading from Bishops Ferry to Williams Kavahaughs Esquire and that his own hands Cap Moores & all the hands that lives on Bartons place work under him.

Ordered that Daniel Allen, Daniel Harpole, Jacob Turney, John Looney, Moses Allen, Isaac Turney, and Peter Little be a Jury to view, mark & lay off a road up the clear fork of Smith fork from John Looneys where the Indian line crosses the same and thath they report the same to our next Court.

Ordered that Samuel Casey, James Smith, Hankerson Rude Greenburry Dixon, John Brownfield, John Gordon, William Hughs be a Jury to view, lay off & mark a road beginning at the Nashville Road near John Wrights on the waters of Smith Fork and extending its course the nearest & best way so as to intersect the river road that leads to Waltons Ferry at the most convenient place.

Ordered that all the hands living convenient to the road lately laid our from Henry Wakefields down the Ridge to the County line work under Stephen Montgomery overseer of the same.

Ordered that William Payne be allowed to keep a Ferry at the mouth of Paytons

Creek.

Ordered on motion that a subpoena Issue to John Williamson to appear at next Court, to say whether he acknowleges a Deed said to be sxecuted by him to Joseph Williamson for 383 acres of Land and that a subpoena issue to William Sullivan Elizabeth Sullivan and Lee Sullivan subscribing witnesses to said Deed In P 101 order to declare whether they say it Sealed & Delivered to the said Joseph.

Ordered that John Brevard, William Sullivan Senr. and Elmore Douglass be appointed Inspectors to the ensuing Election For Governor, Members to Congress to Congress and members of Assembly.

Ordered the Hesekiah Oneil be fined the sum of three dollars for a contempt offered this Court, by ppofanely swearing in their presence & costs.

Ordered that Daniel Alexander be allowed the sum of one dollar & seventy five cents for his services in arresting a certain Mathew Green, and sumoning witnesses and performing other services & C.

Ordered that John Douglass Esqr. be appointed collector of the public& County Taxes for the year 1803 who came into Court gave Security a quallified according to law.

Sampson Williams		
Vs	{	Covenant
Redmund D. Barry		
and		
Sampson Williams		
Vs	{	Case
Redmund D Barry		

In both the above cases ordered that a De. Po. issue to take the Deposition of Robt Searcy "de bone esse, ten days notice to be given the Deft Davidson County- And De. Po. to take the deposition of Wm White Secretary of North Carolina at the Secretaries office in Raleigh thirty days notice to be given the Defendant.

The Court enters up Judgment against the following persons for taxes due & payable on the tracts of land herein after mentioned The owners of which having P 102 failed to return the same for the year 1802

John Smith 1280 acres in two Tracts Round Lick Creek Peter Black 640 acres Round Lick Creek,—Robert Williams 274 acres Mulherins Creek–David Shelton 960 acres round Lick Creek–Daniel Anderson 640 acres Mulherins Creek—Gideon Lamb 5000 acres Round Lick— John Ford 1560 acres Do-Do Samuel Love 1508 Acres Do-Do- Robert King 640 acres adjounning the South & East boundaries of a 1000 acre tract known by the name of Harts Land William Hay 2560 acres four Tracts of640 each on Clendennens Creek—Francis Childs Heirs 3840 acres Caney Fork—William Fireby 3060 acres Situation not known John Allen 3560 acres Caney Fork Stephen Lynn 1000 acres Do-Do— Thomas Campbell 274 acres-Do-Do Archibald Felts 1000 acres

Caney Fork		Baker Archer	640 acres
Do—	do	William Mills	640 acres
Do—	Do	Eilliam Russell	1280 acres
Do—	Do	two Tracts Jacob Adams	640 acres
Do—	Do	John Slow	640 Acres
Do—	DO	Robert Redden	640 acres
Do—	Do	Redmund D. Barry 640 acres	Martins Creek Redmund D. Barry

428 Salt Lick Creek Redmund D. Barry 640 acres Martins Creek- Redmund D. Barry 640 P 103 acres Indian Creek Redmund D Barry 1000 acres South Side Cumberland River John Hall 2560 acres South Side Cumberland River. It is therefore ordered that so much of the aforesaid Lands be condemned by the said Court as will be Sufficient to pay the Taxes and Incidental costs accruing thereon.

The Court Adjourned until Court in Course to meet at the house of William Saunders.

Attest
Sampson Williams

Peter Turney
Thos. Smith
James Roberts
James Draper

At atCourt opened and held for the County of Smith at the house of William Saunders on the third Monday being the nineteenth day of September one thousand eight hundred & three
Present the worshipful
Charles Kavanaugh
Elmore Douglass
James Hibits   Esquires Justices &C
John Lancaster and
Nathaniel Brittain

Ordered that That Thomas Armstrong be excused form further attendance as a Juror during this Term.

Deed 130 acres Samuel Hughs to William Turnbull proven by the oath of James Hibbits one of the subscribing witnesses thereto & ordered to be registered.

P 104   Deed Peter Moore to Charles Mundine 320 acres proven by the oath of James Johnson a subscribing witness thereto and ordered to be registered.

Ordered that Administration of the Estate of Alexander Kenedy deceased be committed to Elizabeth Kennedy and Alexander Cathey, who who thereupon gave security and took oaths prescribed by law.

Deed 120 acres William Saunders to Daniel H. Burford acknowleged and ordered to be registered.

Deed 200 acres Edmund Jennings to Elias Johns acknowleged ordered to be registered.

Daniel H. Burford exhibited his stock mark being two underkeels in ear ordered to be recorded.

Ordered that the report of the Jury who recieved and marked the road from Salt Lick road across Cumberland river at the mouth of Wartrace to the County line be received be received and that George W. Harvey be overseer of the same and that all the hands on Wartrace and Indian Creek work under him.

The following persons were impanneled & sworn as a Grand Jury for the body of this County (towit) David Keighlow, Moses Hart, Isham Beasley, Leonard Ballow, Charles McMurry, William Wooten Jabez, Gifford, John Gray, Patrick Donoho, William Douglass, Phillip Day, George Rowland who having recieved their charge withdrew to consider of their presentments.

William Turnbull records his Took mark tow crops two slits and two under keels in each ear Branding Iron W T.

Ordered that Andrew Goffs tax list for the year 1803 being 754 acres of land in three tracts be received.

Letter of Attorney Sampson Bethel to Cantrell Bethel proven by the oath of Looney Esquire ordered to be recorded.

Joseph Bishop exhibits his Stock mark, being a swallow fork in each ear

Ordered to be recorded.

P 105   Ordered that Amos Lacey and Jeffrey Sutton be appointed patrollers in and for the bounds of Cap Matlock Company and that Daniel Alexander and Samuel Abbots be appointed Patrollers in and for the bounds of Cap Samuels Company.

Ordered that William Hargis be Overseer of the road of which John Rankins was heretofore overseer and that the same hands continue to work upon the same as heretofore.

Ordered that Jesse Smith be overseer of the road of which Leonard Fite (resigned) was formerly overseer and that the same hands continue to work upon the same as heretofore.

Court Adjourned until Tomorrow nine oclock.

Tuesday morning September 20th 1803 Court met according to Adjournment
Present the Worshipful   John Lancaster
                          James Hibbits and   Esquires Justices
                          Elmore Douglass

William Look
    vs   In case upon argument of the rule for a new trial obtained
Joseph Russell   in this cause at the last term. It is considered that the
same be discharged and that the Plaintiff recover against the his damages aforesaid by the said Jury assessed and his costs by him about his suit in this behalf expended and that Defendant in mercy &C.

James W. Wright is appointed a Constable who thereupon gave bond and took the necessary oaths as prescribed by Law.

Ordered in motion of Samuel Stalcup that Alsey Pierce surrender to said Samuel upon his application the Bastard child of said Alseys by name Ele of which the said Samuel is reputed Father and that said Samuel give Security for P 106   the maintenance of the same at the next Court If said Alsey refuses to surrender as aforesaid it is ordered that she shall come forward at the next Court and give Security as aforesaid.

Ordered that William Sullivan Senr. be appointed Overseer of the road of which Robert Rowland is now overseer in his stead.

Archibald Donoho
    vs   In this suit ordered that a De. Po. issue to take the
Sampson Williams   Deposition of Thomas Lacey for the Plaintiff in the
Missippi(Mississippi?) Territory at the house of John Stampley Esquire on the 27th day of November next and that he be sworn on his voir dire.

Ordered that David Soviells be overseer to open and keep in repair the road where David Keighlough was late overseer and that the same hands work under him.

Ordered that Solomon Blair be overseer of the Road in stead of George Tomason resigned, and that the same hands work under him.

Christian Boston
    vs   Appeal
William Kelton   In this case a rule to shew cause why a new
trial should be granted upon argument the above rule was discharged.

Deed 640 acres Joshua Hadley to James Wright proven by the oath Lee Sullivan a subscribing witness thereto Ordered to be Recorded.

Deed 50 acres Joseph Laurence to Zedikiah Ingram proven by the oath of Lee Sullivan one of the subscribing witnesses Ordered to be registered.

Ordered that all the hands below the forks of the road at Bowermans work to Saunders Ferry & that Lewis Mcfarland be Overseer.

P 107   Ordered that William L. Alexander work from Dixons Spring to opposite James Cherrys and that the hands west of that place work under him.

Ordered that John Cage be overseer of the road from opposite Cherrys to Paytons Creek and that all the hands East of that place who formerly worked under him work on on the same.

The Court Adjouned until tomorrow 9 oclock.

Wednesday morning September 21st 1803 - Court met according to adjournment.
Present the worshipful   James Gwin
                          James Hibbits and   Esquires Justices
                          Lee Sullivan

Willis Jones who appears duly commissioned as surveyor in and for the County of Smith bearing date the 15th day of August 1803 came into Court gave Security and took the necessary oaths and als the oath of office (Towit) I, Willis Jones do swear that I well and truly perform all the duties of Surveyor in & for the County of Smith agreeable to Law to the best of my skill and abilities so long as I continue in office so help me God.

Deed Town Lot William Saunders to John L. Martin Acknowleged & ordered to be Registered.

William Payne who heretofore obtained an order for a Ferry on cumberland River at the mouth of Paytons Creek came into Court and entered into bond and Securit

P 108   Ordered that all the Inhabitants of Indian Creek above William Young and the inhabitants on the road from the head of Snow Creek to William Kelleys and Richard Porterfield also James Erwin James & John Pryor work under Henry Bohanon Overseer.

Ordered that all the hands be liable to work on the road from the from the forks of Lancaster road and Waltons to the Indian boundary work on that District of road & that Joseph Shaw be Overseer.

Deed 1000 acres Frederick Debo & John Stoefford to William Hargis Acknowleged & ordered to be registered.

Ordered that Lewis Mcfarland be Overseer to keep in repair the the road in place of Isham Beasley and that the same hands work under him.

Ordered that James Lees Tax list of 596 acres of Land be received and the tax was accordingly paid.

Ordered that Thomas Heaton be appointed constable who came into Court, gave Security & quallified according to Law.

Thomas Wimbs is appointed Constable who came into Court gave Security and quallified according to law.

Ordered that James Hibbits Esquire be exhonorated or have a credit for six dollars & two thirds due to the County Treasurer for a stray horse for which he made a mistake in the return of the appraisments.

Ordered that Execution on a fine levied against Hesekiah Oneil for a contempt offered this Court, be suspended until next Court.

Ordered that James Roberts, James Draper, and Archibald Sloan be commissioners to divide lands of William Young Deceased among the Heirs and to lay off one third to the Widow and relect of the said Deceased.

P 109   The following persons are appointed to serve as Jurors to the ensuing Court (Towit) John Ward, Edward Cage, Moses Pinkston, James Baker, William Stephenson, Daniel Hammock, Jacob Hawick, Nicholas Shrum, Elias Johns William Turnbull, John Brevard, Jeremiah Taylor, Joseph Gifford Aron Hart Fransis Patterson, James Gibson, John Shelton, Grant Allen, Andrew Greer, Abram Thompson, James Montgomery, Joel Hollard, Josiah Howell, William Dillon, Stephen Box, Godfrey Fowler, John Rankin, Thomas Bowman, Robt. Bowman, Joel Dyer, David Cooran, Anthony Samuels, Samuel Evett, and George Matlock.

Ordered that the report of a Jury for a road from the River to Hickmans Creek, be received.

Ordered that Charles Carter, Henry Sadler and William Caldhoun, be overseers to open and keep in repair a road from Waltons road down Martins Creek, to cross Cumberland at the Salt Lick and intersect the Fort Blount road at Poles Mill and that all the hands on Martins Creek and up Cumberland on the South side up to the Salt Lick work under them.

Ordered that the hands allowed Stephen Montgomery to clear out & open a Road from Wakefields down the Ridge be exempted therefrom and that they work under their former Overseer.

Ordered that John Gordon be overseer to open & keep in repair a road layed out by a Jury from the River side road to Hickmans creek and that Thomas Smith Esqr. furnish said Overseer with a list of hands.

Ordered that Edward Brownfield be Overseer to open and keep in repair a road from Hickmans Creek, to the Nashville Road and that Thomas Smith Esquire furnish him with a list of hands.

Letter of Attorney John Miles to Samuel Miles acknowleged in open Court. Ordered to be Registered.

P 110   John Douglass Esquire Sheriff & Collector for the County of Smith made report to Court that the following Lands returned for taxation for the year 1802 be found no property on which he could distrain (To wit)
John Davidson - 168 Acres
Thomas Hamilton 1280 acres
John Buchanon - 640 Acres,
George Laurnece 1000 Ditto
John Khun(?) 274 Do
Thos. Love 1000 Do
Levi Sanderlin 100 Do
Charles Marshall 320 Do
Thomas Taylor 640 Do
Abraham Moore 320 Do
John Kenedy 320 Do
John Nichols 1097 Do
William Laurence 333 Do
Eqhraim Payton 1280 Do
Thomas Farmer 640 Do
Henry Rowan 540 Do
Thomas Farmer 640 Do
Thos. Woodiffs (Woodriff) Heirs 320 Do

Richard Goham (Garham?) 519 Do
William Walters - 2011 Do
William Henderson 640 Do
Nath. Browns heirs 640 Do
Jas & John Banner (Bonner?) 3292 Do
Robert Hays 4880 Do -
Do - Do 1097 Do
Stockley Hays 1280 Do -
Do Do 640 Do
Thomas Persons heirs 4800 Do -
Do Do Do 640 Do
Richard Cross 1000 Do
Robert Fenner - 1920 De
Sherrold Green 1000 Do Lewis Gutridge. It is therefore ordered that the foregoing
lands be twice published in the Tennessee Gazette and once in the Knoxville Gazette
giving notice that the same will be sufficient to pay the tax and Incidental costs
accruing thereon.

William Anderson records his Stock mark being two swallow forks.

Court Adjourns until Court in course to meet at the House of Tilman Dixon.
S. Williams Clk.   Thomas Smith
                                                       John Lancaster
                                                       Nath. Brittain

P 111   At a Court opened & held for the County of Smith on Monday the 19th of
December 1803 at Tilman Dixons Spring Members present :viz: The Worshipful
                              Charles Kavanaugh
                              Elmore Douglass   Esquires Justices &C
                              Arthur Hogan and
                              John Lancaster

Deed Thomas Masten
      To
Henry Hyde   640 acres of land proven by the oath of George Smith
a subscribing witness thereto and ordered to be Registered.

Deed William Head
      To
Andrew Greer   640 acres of land proven by the oath of William L.
Lawson a subscribing witness thereto & ordered to be registered.

Letter of Attorney John Miles to Thomas Parsons proven by the oath of Daniel
Burford a subscribing witness thereto and ordered to be registered.

Deed Solomon Harpole to John Harris 228 acres of land proven by the oath of
Charles A. Burton a subscribing witness thereto and ordered to be registered.

The last Will & testament of Daniel Mingle was produced in Court and proven
by Oliver Layson David Williams and William Kearby & ordered to be recorded.

Whereupon Abgail(?) Mingle widow & relect of the said deceased came into Court
into Court and expessed (expressed) her dissent to the last will and Testament of
the said deceased & expressed her resolution to abide by the provisions provided her
by the law out of her said Deceased husbands estate John Con John Brevard and James
Hibits nominated as Executors of the aforesaid will came into Court & quallified
accordingly.

The last will and Testament of Peter Starbuck was produced into Court and
proven by the oath of Lewis Wimberly and Isaac Dillon Subscribing witnesses thereto

P. 112 and ordered to be recorded And thereupon came into Josiah Howell one of the persons named in the will and testament as Executors of the same and quallified accordingly.

Deed of conveyance from John Williamson Senior of Smith County & State of Tennessee to Joseph Williamson of the County of Montgomery & state of Verginia for three hundred & eighty three acres of land in the County of Montgomery aforesaid on the South Side of Back Creek a branch of New River dated the 15th day of May in the year Eighteen hundred was acknowleged in open Court by the aforesaid John Williamson to be the act & deed of the said John Williamson and it was ordered by the Court that the Clerk certify on a Schedule anexed to said Deed a transfer of the record of this order in due form in order that the said Deed may be recorded in the County & State where the lands contained in said Deed lies.

Augustine Cook security security for the appearance of Josiah Payne came into Court & surrendered him up in discharge of himself ordered into the custody of the Sheriff.

The Administration of the Estate of Edward Donoho deceased was committed to Richard Brittain who thereupon intered into Bond for the due purformance thereof in the sum of five thousand dollars with William Martin and Charles Donoho his Securities And the said Richard Brittain Administrator as aforesaid in open Court took the oaths prescribed by law.

James Tremble Esquire produced his license as an attorney at Law took the necessary oaths and thereupon is admitted to practice in this Court.

Washing L. Hannum(?) Esquire produced his License as an attorney at Law took the necessary oaths and thereupon is admitted to practice in this.

An Inventory of the Sale of the Estate of Alexander Kenedy was returned into Court & ordered to be recorded.

P. 113 . Grand Jury drawn impannelled, sworn and charged, to wit) Grant Allen foreman William Turnbull Abram Thompson Joel Holland, Joel Dyer, John Rankins, John Barkley, Jeremiah Taylor John Ward Daniel Hammock James Gibson, Nicholas Shrum and Joseph Gifford John Kavanaugh Constable Sworn to attend the Grand Jury who withdrew to consider of presentments & Indictments.

James Draper, James Gwin, John Gordon, Joseph Collens and Henry Tooley Commissioners for fixing the public Buildings came into Court and entered into bond & quallified according to law.

Deed 222 acres Robert King to David Young proven by the oath of James Vance one of the Subscribing witnesses.

Job Bass records his stock mark and Brand The mark being both ears cropped & an under bit in each and a slit in the right ear Brand J. B.

Ordered that Samuel Hannah be overseer of the Sams road where Washington Harney was late overseer & that the same hands work thereon as were heretofore liable.

Richard Lancaster came into Court and resigned his appointment as Overseer of the road and William Powell is appointed in his stead the same hands to work under him as was liable to work under the late Overseer.

Deed of Gift Nathan Jackson to Polley Jackson & Robert Lancaster Proven by the oath of Daniel Jackson one of the subscribing witnesses Let it be recorded.

The following persons appeared in Court produced their commissions as con-

servators of the peace for Smith County and Quallified according to law (To wit)
James vance James
P114 Rolstone, John Gordon, Junior, Gideon Pillow, Martin Young, Alexander
Henry, Bashal Shaw, Godfrey Fowler Aaron Hart, Josiah Howell James Cotton Wilson
Gage and Archibald Sloane, Commissioners bearing date the 7th of November 1803
who thereupon took their Seats.

Ordered that Robert Ward be overseer of the road in place of William Payne
and that the same hands work under him as were liable to work under the late overseer.

Ordered that Jacob Johnson be Overseer of the road in place of John Jinkins re-
signed and that the same hands work under him as was liable to work under the late
Overseer and that the said road be opened & kept in repair the new way across Defeated
Creek Hill as lately laid out by a Jury.

Ordered that Doctor Jennings be overseer of the road in place of Stephen Box
resigned and that the same hands work under him as were heretofore liable to work
on said road.

Ordered that Solomon Thomas be Overseer of the Road in place of James Kitchen
resigned and that the same hands work under him.

Deed 333 1/3 acres George Laurence to William Laurence proven by the oath of
Arthur H. Hogan one of the subscribing Witnesses thereto. Let it be registered.

Deed 95 acres Henry W. Lawson to Mathew Harper proven by the oath of Zaddock
McNew one of the subscribing witnesses thereto.

Deed 95 acres Henry W. Lawson to Enos Harrold proven by the oath of Mathew
Harper one of the subscribing witnesses thereto.

Deed 158 Acres Edward Gwin to Robert Box proven by the oath of Stephen Box
one of the subscribing witnesses thereto.

Court then Adjourned until Tomorrow nine oclock.

P 115   Tuesday December 20th 1803 - Court met according to adjournment
Members present :Viz: The Worshipful Tilman Dixon,
                                       Charles Kavanaugh
                                       John Lancaster &   Esquires Justices &
                                       Archibald Sloane

Ordered that the Administrators of the Estate of Nathan Jackson. Deceased be
committed to the care of Daniel Jackson who came into Court gave security & qualified
according to law.

Deed 151 acres John Sedgley to Elisha Oglesby proven by the oath of William
Sampson one of the subscribing witnesses.

Ordered that Richard Lancaster be constable in John Lancasters District who
came into Court gave Security and Quallified according to Law.

Abegail Mungle Petition for Dower. Ordered that the Sheriff be directed to
summon a Jury of good & lawful men to lay off said Dower and that the Clerk issue
his writ accordingly.

Ordered that John Brevard be appointed Guardian to Isaac Mungle who made
choice of him in open Court and who was approved of by the Court and the said John
Brevard came into Court gave bond with Peter Turney & Andrew Greer his securities
& quallified according to law. And the Court consisting of Tilman Dixon James Hibbits

Archibald Sloan Aaron Hart and John Lancaster all approved of the Guardian.

Ordered that David Rorix be constable in Captain Matlocks Company who came into Court gave security and quallified according to law.

Ordered that Alen Wilkerson Overseer of the Road from Michael Murphys to the foot of the ridge leading to Daniel Witchers and that Peter Turney Esquire give said Overseer a list of hands.

Ordered that William Jenkins be Overseer to open & keep in repair a road from the foot of the ridge to Daniel Witchers & that Marlin Young Esquire furnish said Overseer with a list of hands.

The last will and Testament of William Saunders Deceased was exhibited in court and was proven by the oath of Daniel Burford and Redmond D. Barry two of the subscribing witnesses thereto both of whom also swore they saw William Alexander subscribe his name as a witness at the same time and the said Redmond D. Barry also swore that the said Deceased directed him to sign his name to the Codicil to said will and Nancy Saunders Widow & relect of said Deceased came into Court and qualified according to Law.

Court Adjournment until Tomorrow 9 oclock -

Wednesday December 21st 1803 Court met according to adjournment
Present   Peter Turney
          John Lancaster and   Esquires Justices
          John Looney

Ordered that a Subpoena Issue to summon William Sullivan Junior to appear at our next Court of Pleas & Quarter Sessions to be held for this County on the second Monday in March next then & there to declare on oath whether he saw William Sullivan Senior Sign Seal and deliver a Deed of conveyance to John Williamson and whether he became a subscribing to said Deed.

P 117   The Grand Jury into Court the following Presentments one against James Tremble for profane swearing the other other against John Hargis whereupon the Court discharged the Jury &C.

Samuel Comer produced the Bond of William Saunders in open Court and the same was proven by the oath of of James Curtis one of the subscribing witnesses thereto.

Deed 220 acres Samuel Comer to Richard Condry proven by the oath of James Curtis one of the subscribing witnesses.

Ordered that John Williamson be Overseer to open & keep in repair a road laid out by a Jury from Williamsons Ferry to Sullivans road and that the following hands work under him, To wit, his own Micajah Duke Robert Brooks Zignal Cook & Edward Barbee.

Deed 320 acres Executors of William Saunders to Samuel Comer acknowleged by James Sanders and ordered to be registered.

William Penny appointed Constable in Cap Samuels Company who came into Court gave Bond & Security and quallified according to law.

Richard Reynolds appointed Overseer of the road in the place of James Vance and the same hands to work under him.

Deed 1280 acres Reuben Cage Sheriff to Micajah Barrow proven by the oath of Jesse Wharton one of the subscribing witnesses thereto.

Ordered that a Sci. fa. Issue to revive a Judgment obtained by Hesekiah ⬛⬛ against James Moore Heirs Ordered that John Kavanaugh be appointed Constable for Smith County who gave Bond and security & qualified as the law directs.

118   Ordered that Stephen Montgomery, John Brevard William Turnbull Aaron ⬛⬛ Samuel Corruthers, George Anderson & Joel Holland be a Jury to view a road ⬛⬛ near Coruthers Horse Mill the nearest and best way up the East fork of Goose ⬛⬛ until it intersect the Kentucky road, leading by James Gwins at the most convenient place and that they report the same to our next Court.

Ordered that Court adjoun until tomorrow nine oclock.

Tuesday December the 22nd 1803 Court met according to Adjournment - Members present (To wit) William Walton ⎤
                                    John Lancaster   ⎪
                                    Tilman Dixon   ⎬ Esquires Justices &C.
                                    Arthur S. Hogan and ⎪
                                    John Gordon Junior ⎦
appeared & took their seats Ordered that Vincent Ridley be Overseer of the road in place of Godfrey Fowler and that the same hands work under him.

Deed 44 0 acres Robert Campbells Heirs To John Campbell proven by the oath of Alexander McKee one of the subscribing witnesses thereto.

Deed 200 acres Alexander McKee to Alexander Donaldson and Thomas Jefferson Williams Acknowleged in open Court.

Ordered that John McGee's and Charles Ledbetters hands work from Dixons Lick Creek to the ford of Dixons Creek on the fort Blount road.

Ordered that Gideon Pillow, William Walton, John Gordon Junior, John Lancaster & Thomas Smith Esquires or any two of them be commissioners to take such Depositions may be thought necessary to perpetuate Testimony to establish a location and grant in the name of Samuel Ash for 2560 acres of Land lying on Mulherins Creek and other specialties called for in said Location & Groent and that a subpoena Issue to compel P 119 the attendence of said witness and such examination to be taken in writing signed by the witnesses and attested by the said commissioners which Depositions to be Transmitted to the Clerk of this Court on or before the second Monday in March next which examination is to be taken on the premises &C.

Ordered that a road be viewed laid off & marked from where the Wilson Road strikes the Smith County line near Round Lick Creek the nearest & best way to near the mouth of Hickmans Creek and that the following persons view, lay off & mark the same :viz: William Smith, William Hankins Harris Bradford Joseph Prewitt, James Cotten Leonard Caplinger and Wilson Coats and make report to our next Court.

Ordered that Nicholas Matlocks tax list of 426 acres of land be received which Tax was paid.

Ordered that Hugh Stephen be appointed Overseer of the road in place of Henry Dancer and that the same hands work under him.

Ordered that John Gordon Junior & Gideon Pillow Esqrs. divide the hands liable to work on public roads among the following Overseers (To wit) Mathew Payne, Enos Harroad, Zaddock McNew, Edward Bromfield and John Gordon Junior.

Ordered that the road from Boling Felts to the Nashville road be Discontinued and the hands of said Road work under Jesse Smith.

Court Adjourns until Court in course to meet at the of William Walton.

Williams Clk.

           W. Walton
           John Lancaster
           T. Dixon
           James Gwin

120   At a Court opened & held for the County of Smith on Monday the 12th of March 1804 at the house of William William Walton. Members present, To wit, Worshipful   Charles Kavanaugh
                    Lee Sullivan
                    Arthur Hogan
                    Godfrey Fowler   Esquires Justices &C.
                    Archibald Sloane and
                    Aaron Hart

Deed 200 acres Arthur A. Hogan to Cornelius Waggoner acknowleged.

Deed 640 acres Lewis Green to Joseph Sitton proven by the oath of Jeremiah Peek one of the subscribing witnesses Let it be recorded.

Deed 100 Acres Stephen Montgomery to Aaron Hart proven by the oath of Jabez Gifford one of the subscribing witnesses thereto Let it be recorded.

Deed 240 Acres Stephen Montgomery to Jabez Gifford proven by the oath of Aaron Hart one of the subscribing witnesses thereto Let it be registered.

Ordered that the report of the Jury who viewed the road from near Coruthers Horse Mill up the // east Fork of Goose Creek be received and that William Turnbull be overseer to open and keep the same in repair from the forks near said Horse Mill to Jabez Giffords and that all the hands below said Giffords on said fork work under him and that Andrew ford be Overseer from said Giffords to Stephen Montgomerys and that all the hands living above said Giffords up as high as Stephen Montgomerys work under him. And that George Anderson be overseer from said Montgomerys to Gwins road and that the long Creek and Ridge hands work under him.

P 121   John Page exhibits his stock mark being a crop off the left ear and under bit in the right ear and Brand P and the same is recorded.

Ordered that in the suit James Vance against Armistead Stubblefield the Writ be so amended as to changed from debt to covenant on th Plaintiffs paying the cost.

Ordered that Richard Taylor and James Bermingham each be bound in the sum of two hundred dollars payable payable to the chairman of Smith County Court and his Successors in office to be void in condition that they or either of them indemnified from any charge that may hereafter be bought for the maintenance of a Base born child which Godfrey Jones is the reputed Father of and that they maintain and Educate said child as well as is common Whereupon the said Richard Taylor & James Bermingham came into Court and acknowleged themselves bound as aforesaid.

Deed 1000 acres Turner Harwood to William Murphy proven by the oath of William Boren one of the subscribing witnesses.

Ordered that so much of the land of David King be condemned as will satisfy a Judgment for one dollar cost due to William Short as appears by a Judgment Obtaine before Aaron Hart Esquire on the eleventh of February 1804 Together with the accruing cost.

Ordered that so much of the Lands & Tenements of David King be condemned as will satisfy a Judgment obtained by John Sullivan before Nathaniel Brittain Esquire on the 3d day of January 1804 Together with the accruing cost.

On motion John H. Bowen Esquire who produced his as an Attorney at Law, is mitted to practice in this Court who took the necessary oaths.

122   William Marchbanks & Lewis Ford Esquires both of whom appears duly
commissioned as Justices of the peace by a commission bearing date the 7th day
1803 came into Court & took the oath prescribed by Law.

Court Adjourns until Tomorrow nine oclock..

Tuesday March 13th 1804 Court met according to adjournment. Members present
to wit, The Worshipful   Peter Turney
                         Elmore Douglas
                         James Roberts   Esquires Justices
                         James Draper and
                         William Marchbanks

Ordered that Charles Carter be allowed to administer on the estate of John
Carter Deceased who came into Court and entered into bond with Edward Hogan &
William Anderson his securities and quallified according to law.

Ordered that James Gwin Esquire be allowed a credit of four dollars sixty
six & two third cents in his settlement with the commissioners to settle with the
County Trustee &C.

Ordered that Moses Griffin be Overseer of that part of the road where John
Gage was Overseer and the same hands to work under him, that worked under the
late Overseer.

Ordered that James Gwin Esquire be appointed County Trustee who came into
Court gave security & quallified according to Law.

Ordered that James Draper Esquire be County Commissioner in and for the
County of Smith who came into court and qualified according to Law.

P 123   Bill of Sale Brewning B. Williams to Morgan Williams proven by the oath
of Duke Williams one of the subscribing witnesses.

On the affidavit of Daniel Bridgman ordered that a De.Po. issue to take the
Depositions of Ezekiel Ray & wife Druella and David White de bene esse in the suit
said Bridgman against Freeman Bufrow and Nathaniel Brittain Ten days notice to be
given the Defendants.

Bond John Bridges To Rebeccah Moore Acknowleged in open Court.

Deed 180 Acres Robert King to Jacob Fanning proven by the oath of James
Galey one of the subscribing witnesses.

The following persons were are appointed to serve as Jurors to the next
Superior Court, To wit, Andrew Greer, Joseph Collens John Vantrice, and Joel
Dyer Junior.

Ordered that Joseph Prewit be Overseer to open & keep in repair a road from
the Wilson County line to the first crossing of Mulherins Creek and that James
Cotton Esquire furnish said overseer with a list of hands.

Ordered that Henry Tooley one of the commissioners appointed to settle with
the County Trustee be allowed the sum of two dollars for his services &C.

Ordered that Thomas Smith Esquire be overseer to open and keep in repair a
road as lately layed out by a Jury from the ford of Mulherins Creek where Joseph

grewit quits work to where it intersects Kavanaughs Road near said Smiths and
what John Gordon Esquire furnish said with a list of hands.

Ordered that John Stone be appointed Constable who came into Court entered
into Bond with security and Qualified according to Law.

P 124   Ordered that all the hands who formerly worked on the road from Bishops
Ferry to Williams Kavanaughs work under Thomas Banks.

Ordered that Joel Dyer Junr. be overseer to work on that part of the Road
leading up Paytons Creek from the corner of old Mr. Pipers fence to Michael Murphys and that the said hands work under him agreeable to the division made by
Ibram Piper & said Dyer.

Lee Sullivan Esquire offered his resignation as a Justice of the Peace in
open Court and the same is entered of record.

The following persons were appointed to serve as Jurors to the next Court,
To wit, Daniel Hammonk, John Gray, James Bradley, John Warren, Jacob Dice, Thomas
Banks James Caps Booker Bradford James Jenkins, Moses Justice, William Jarrol,
Jacob Fenner, William Douglass, Charles McMurry, Jeffrey Sitton, Willeroy Pate,
Henry Huddleston, William Wooten, William Lane, Samuel Casey, Zaddock McNew,
James Ballow, Pleasant Kearby, Thomas Draper Jesse Laurence James Montgomery,
Edward Settles, George Tomason, William Farris Junior, Thomas Williamson, Michael
Murphy, Andrew Greer, Richard Brittain, Henry Dancer, Henry Sadley, Thomas Bowman,
Isham Beasley, John Barkley, and John Shelton.

Ordered that Tellitha Smith be bound in the sum of two hundred dollars for
the maintenance of a Base born child begotten on her body by the name of William
whereupon the the said Tillitha Smith came into Court and acknowleged herself
bound as aforesaid with Daniel Mitchal her security who paid the sum of three
dollars twelve & a half cents as a fine & two dollars & fifty cents as a fee
to the County Solicitor.

P 125   Ordered that the Clerk issue execution against the Estate of William
Saunders Deceased in the suit John Morris against said Saunders it being certified to said Court that said suit was dismissed in the Superior Court and re-
manded to this Court.

Ordered that the balance of hands remaining in this County who were heretofore liable to work under Elijah Gadda, who has lately fallen into Wilson County,
in future work under Charles Kavanaugh and that he work to the Wilson line.

Deed 182 acres Arthur A. Hogan to James Hodges acknowleged.

An Inventory account of the Estate of Daniel Mingle Deced. returned into
Court by James Hibbits one of the Executors ordered to be recorded.

Deed 250 acres William Sullivan Senior to John Williamson proven by the
oath of William Sullivan Junior one of the subscribing witnesses.

Recognizance of John Morris who stands charged with begetting a Bastard
child on the body of Nelly Gasway returned into Court.

Deed Arthur Hogan to Thomas Hall for 98 acres Acknowleged in open Court.

An Inventory account of the Estate of William Sanders Deceased returned
into Court by Charles Burton ordered to be recorded.

Bond John Bridges James Moore & Alfred Moore To Hesekiah Oneil proven by
the oath of John Chambers the subscribing witness.

An Inventory account of the Estate of Nathan Jackson returned into Court Daniel Jackson the administrator ordered to be Recorded.

126   An Inventory account of Sales of the Estate of Peter Starbuck Deceased returned into Court by Josiah Howell one of the Executors ordered to be recorded.

Deed 200 acres Rebeckah Moore to John Bridges proven by the oath of Hezekiah Oneil one of the subscribing witnesses thereto.

Court Adjourns until Tomorrow eight oclock.

Wednesday March the 14th 1804 Court met according to adjournment - Members present (To Wit) The Worshipful   Charles Kavanaugh }
                                      William Walton   }
                                      Arthur Hogan   }
                                      John Patterson   }   Esquires Justices &C.
                                      Willis Jones   }
                                      John Gordon and) }
                                      John Looney   }

The papers relative to the Division of the Lands of William Young Deceased Among the Heirs & Devesees of said Deceased was returned into Court Ordered to be recorded.

Ordered that Richard Banks Andrew Greer, and Thomas Smith, be appointed to settle with the County Trustee and that such Settlement be returned into the next County Court.

Deed 333 1/3 acres William Laurence To William Walton proven by the oath of Arthur Hogan one of the subscribing witnesses.

Deed 150 3/4 acres William Walton to Benjamin John's acknowleged in open Court Let it be registered.

P 127   Ordered that James Haynie be appointed Overseer of the road from Sullivans Ferry to the Fort Blount road and that the same hands work on the same as was heretofore liable to work under the late Overseer.

Court Adjourns until Court in Course to meet at the house of Peter Turney.
Test   Charles Kavanaugh
S. Williams   John Lancaster
                                                    John Gordon

P 128   At a Court opened & held from the County Smith at the late dwelling house of Peter Turney Deceased on Monday the 11th day of June 1804. Members Present (To wit) The Worshipful   Tilman Dixon   }
                                      Godfrey Fowler   } Esquires Justices &C
                                      James Vance   }

The following persons from the original venire returned to this Term, were drawn, Elected, tried & sworn & charged as a Grand Jury to this Term, Towit, Andrew Greer, foreman, Michael Murphy, John Gray, Thomas Bowman, William Wooten, George Thomason, William Lane, Richard Brittain, Charles McMurry, Edward Settes, James Bradley, James Jinkins, Thomas Draper, Samuel Casey, James Cope, William Penny a Constable sworn to attend them.

Deed 640 Acres, James Robertson to William Trigg Junr. Proven by the oath of Andrew Greer a subscribing witness thereto and ordered to be registered.

Leonard Ballow exhibits his stock mark being a crop and a slit in the right ear & swallow fork in the left ordered to be recorded.

John Barkley & Henry Sadler are excused from attending on the Venire at this term.

Bennett H. Henderson Esquire produced his Licence an an Attorney at Law and on motion is admitted to practice in this Court who thereupon took the oaths prescribed by Law.

P 129   Joseph Williams exhibits his Stock mark in open Court being a crop off both ears, & two slits in each and the same is recorded.

Ordered that George Matlock & Godfrey Fowler Esquires be Commissioners to settle with William Martin relative to his Guardianship for John Young and such Settlement when made return into our next Court.

Ordered that Patrick Donoho be Overseer of the road in place of John Johnson resigned and that the same hands work thereon as heretofore.

Ordered that the following hands work under Allen Wilkerson Overseer of a road (To wit) John Sloane, John Patterson, Archibald Wilkerson, Benjamin Payne, George Thomason, and John Thomasson.

Charles Carter comes into Court, and relinquishes his right of administration to the Estate of John Carter deceased and Dale Carter produced in Court a regularly authenticated copy of said John Charles will, which said will was admitted to Record - And said Dale Carter being named Sole Executor of said will came into Court and took the oath prescribed by Law as Executor of the Will aforesaid and returned an Inventory of the goods & Chattles belonging to the Estate of said John Carter deceased and thereupon the Court ordered that the perishable property of the said Decedant be sold according to Law.

Ordered that Freeman Burrow be appointed Constable who came into Court gave Security & quallified according to Law.

P 130   Deed 207 acres John Braly to Jacob Overall proven by the oath of adam dale a subscribing witness thereto.

Ordered that Leonard Fite have the previlage of building a water Grist Mill on Smiths fork of the Caney fork he being the owner of the lands on both sides of the River & that he be allowed the customary toll for grinding.

Deed 250 Acres Stockley Donelson to William Reid heirs proven by the oath of Miles Stephens a subscribing witness.

Deed 50 acres Stockley Donelson to William Reid heirs proven by the oath of Miles Stephens a subscribing witness.

David Shelby records his stock mark, (to wit) a Smooth crop in the right ear and a slit in the left also his Brand thus S.

Deed 237 acres Thomas Harney to Thomas Hammock Acknowleged in open Court Ordered to be registered.

Ordered that Adam Deal (Dale) Esquire be allowed the customary rates for grinding at his Mill already built on Smiths fork.

Ordered that Jacob Overall have leave to build a grist Mill and Saw Mill on Smiths fork of the Caney fork it being suggested that he owns the lands on both sides of the Stream aforesaid but upon this express condition that he does not dam up the water so as to injure the Mill already granted to Leonard Fite and that he be authorized to receive the customary Toll.

Court adjourns until tomorrow morning nine oclock.

Tuesday morning June 12th 1804 Court met according to adjournment.
present the Worshipful   John Lancaster
                       Godfrey Fowler and   Esquires Justices &C
                       Archibald Sloane

P 131   Deed 320 acres Martin Armstrong to John Johnson was proven by the oath of Tilman Dixon a subscribing witness ordered to be registered.

Deed for 220 acres Martin Armstrong to Jesse Beasley was proven by the oath of Tilman Dixon a subscribing witness thereto.

Deed 100 acres Martin Armstrong to John Rankin was proven by the oath of Tilman Dixon a subscribing witness thereto let it be Registered.

Deed 220 acres Edmond Jenning to James Ballow acknowleged in open Court.

John Fishers record his stock mark, To wit, a smooth crop off the right ear.

Cap Charles Kavanaugh be appointed Guardian to andrew Johnson Kavanaugh of fourteen years of age, who made choice of him as his Guardian which choice was approved of by the Court and the said Charles Kavanaugh came into Court and entered into Bond with Leonard Fite and Adam Dale his securities for his faithful Guardianship.

Deed for 120 acres Charles Mundine to Hugh McCennin proven by the oath of Charles McCennin a subscribing witness thereto Let it be Registered.

Power of Attorney Stockley Donelson to James Taylor & Henry Bohannan Taylor proven in open Court by the oath of Samuel Walker a subscribing witness thereto ordered to be recorded.

Deed for 100 acres James Pryor to John Dillard proven by the oath of Henry Sellars a subscribing witness thereto.

P 132   Deed for 100 acres John Sedgley to Edward Cage proven by the oath of King Karr a subscribing witness.

Letter of Attorney Claibourn Duval to Buckner Russell Proven by the oath of Martin Young a Subscribing witness.

Ordered that a Supplementary return of the Estate of Daniel Mingle Deceased be received & the same is received and ordered to be recorded.

The Grand Jury returned into Court, & returned a Bill of Indictment against Robert Stuart and withdrew to consider of other Indictments & presentments.

Deed 200 Acres Sampson Williams to Henry Buddleston Acknowleged in open Court.

Henry Wakefield records his stock mark being a crop and a slit in the left ear and an under keel in the right.

Henry Webster records his stock mark being two crops & two slits in each ear.

Martin Young records his stock mark being a swallow fork and over keel in each ear.

Deed 200 acres James Ballow to Stephen Anderson acknowleged in open Court.

The last Will and Testament of Peter Turney Deceased was produced in Court, and offered for probate And and thereupon William Martin one of the subscribing witnesses thereto came into Court proved the due execution thereof who also Swore that Edmond Burton whose name also appears as a subscribing witness subscribed the same as such at the same time with himself and it is thereupon ordered to be recorded - And Sampson Williams one of the Executors therein named came into Court and Qualified as Executor of said will agreeable to the Tenor thereof And the said William Martin the other executor named in the sad will came into Court p 133 & relinquished his right of Executorship.

Deed of Lease William Martin to Daniel Burford acknowleged in open Court.

The Jury Summoned by the Sheriff to lay off the Dower of the Dower of Abegail Mingle & relect of Daniel Mingle Deceased made return thereof which is ordered to be filed as of Record.

The Grand Jury returned into Court & returned a Bill of Indictment against Enos Harrold for an Assault & Battery & withdrew to consider of other indictments and Presentments.

Ordered that Samuel Hannah have the previlege of keeping a water Grist Mill, that he hath already built on Wartrace Creek & that he be allowed the customary Toll for grinding.

Deed 40 acres Henry Tooley to James Gwin Joseph Collins & Henry Tooley Commissioners & acknowleged in open Court Ordered to be Registered.

Ordered that Elisha Dillard have letters of administration on the Estate of John Dilliard Deceased who came into Court gave security and qualified according to law.

The following persons are appointed to serve on the Venire to the next Superior Court, To wit; John L. Martin Grant Alle, William Alexander & William Lancaster.

Ordered that John Douglass be released from paying the Tax on 494 acres of land for the year 1803 & that a copy of this order be a sufficient voucher for the collector.

P 134   Ordered that John Kavanaugh be allowed the sum of nine dollars for his services & expenditures in taking John Anderson to Nashville & for other services rendered the State in summoning witnesses.

Ordered that James Gwin Esquire County Trustee be exhonerated from paying ten dollars for a Stray taken by John Payne in his lifetime and which appears to be proven from him by Charles Carter.

The following persons are appointed to serve on the Grand & Petit Juries to September Term 1804, Towit, John Johnson Hatter, William Brandon, William Roper, David Venters, John Rutherford, Leonard Ballow, Elias Johns, Job Bass, Armistead Moore, William Sullivan Junior, Judd Strother, John Gordon Senr. Benjamin Johns, Joseph Collins, William Martin, Edward Parrish(or Farriss), John Hargis, Henry Tooley, Randal Bren(?),Daniel McFarland, Jonah Woods, Malcom Henry, Stephen Box, Stephen Montgomery, Lewis Pepkin, William Turnbull, John Johnson (Horse Mill) James Smith, Abram Brittain, Benjamin Payne, Christian Boston, William Granade, Boling Felts, John Felts, Henry Wakefield, William Jenkins, Robert Collier, Charles Mundine and Neil Thompson.

Court Adjourns untill Tomorrow nine oclock.

Wednesday morning June 13th 1804 Court met according to adjournment Members

Present (To wit)   James Draper
                    Godfrey Fowler and   Esquires Justices &C
                    James Vance

P 155   Ordered that James Galey & Reubin Goad each be appointed Constable for the ensuing two years both of whom respectively came into Court gave Security qualified according to law.

Letter of Attorney James Moore Whilliam White proven by the oath of Daniel Burford a subscribing witness thereto.

Ordered that Jacob Dice have Letters of administration on the Estate of George Noggle who came into Court gave security & quallified according to Law.

Ordered that John Douglass Esquire late Sheff. be allowed the sum of Eighty Dollars for his exoficio services for the year 1803 and until the second Monday in March 1804.

Ordered that the Clerk be allowed the sum of forty dollars for his Exo ficio services for the year 1803 and that he be allowed the twenty one dollars for his Exo ficio services for the year 1801.

Ordered that two dollars for each Wolf Scalp, be allowed to each person who may kill a Wolf on due proof being made that such Wolfe was killed in this County since the year 1801 and until the 1803.

The Grand Jury came into Court and returned the Bills of Indictment, To wit) one against one against John Young one against Daniel Bridgman one against Nathaniel Brittain one against John Johns one against James Fisher and one against Willy Trumblin and withdrew to consider of other Indictments and Presentments.

Daniel Witcher records his stock mark being a half and under bit in each ear.

P 156   Ordered that the Tax list for the year 1804 returned by James Draper Esquire Commissioner of the revenue be received & the same was received and approved of by the Court.

Ordered that Joseph Price be appointed Guardian to Elizabeth Coger an orphan child of fourteen years of age who has of her own clase(?) chosen him, which choice has been approved of by the Court and the said Joseph Price came into Court & entered into Bond with Joel Dyer & Edward Gwin his securities for his faithful Guardianship.

Deed 50 Acres Samuel Comer to James Laxton proven by the oath of Alexander Lawey one of the subscribing witnesses.

Deed 62½ acres Samuel Thompson to to Chisley Wheeler Acknowleged in open Court.

Deed 62½ acres Samuel Thompson to Robert Cannon acknowleged in open Court.

Ordered that Elisha Dillard be allowed to build a mill on his Spring Branch near Lancaster Ferry and that he be allowed the customary rates of Toll for Grinding.

Ordered that Obediah Saunders be fined fifty cents for a contempt offered this Court and that he remain in custody of the Sheriff until paid.

Court Adjourns until Tomorrow nine oclock.

Thursday morning June the 14th 1804 Court met according to adjournment.

Presents The Worshipful   William Waton
                      John Lancaster
                      Lewis Ford and   Esquires Justices
                      John Gordon

P 157   Ordered that Gideon Pillow be Overseer of the road leading from the Caney Fork to Mulherins Creek and that the following hands work under him, To wit, Martin Hoover, John Hoover, Christopher Hoover, Old Mr. Hoovers hands Dudley Jolly, Alexander McDonald and John Glyze.

Ordered that Vincent Ridley and William L. Alexander be allowed the sum of twenty one dollars & twenty cents for their Trouble and expenses in taking Michae Murphy from his own house to Nashville as a Prisoner and that a copy of this order be a Sufficient voucher for the County Trustee to pay the same.

The Grand Jury came into Court and returned a Bill of Indictment against John Dickson and withdrew to consider of other Indictments & Presentments.

Ordered that James Gwin and Lazarus Cotton be Released from paying for Stray hoggs taken up by Cotten, & was proven away by William Walon (?) as his property And that the said James Gwin be allowed a credit for the sum due said County for said Stray Hoggs ordered that a road be viewed layed off and marked from Arthur Hogans Esquires to Mr. Robert Wards and that William Wooten, William Lane, Richard Rizen, Thomas Hale and Jeremiah Hale view the same and make report to to our ensuing Court.

Ordered that Anthony Samuels be appointed Overseer of that part of the road where William Alexander was late overseer and the same hands to work under him.

P 158   Ordered that James Bradley be overseer of the road from Bledsoesborough, to the intersection of the Bledsoes road and the road leading from Banks's ferry to John Sheltons and the hands who were heretofore liable to work on said road continue to work to work thereon.

Ordered that the following hands work from Dixons Lick Creek to the Fork of Dixons Creek on the Fort Blount road, To wit, Tilman Dixons hands, John Johnson, Joseph Lock Samuel Evetts and John Moore & that Elisha Thomas be Overseer of the same.

Ordered that James Gwin, Henry Tooley, and Joseph Collens Commissioner be allowed the sum of Ten Dollars for James Sampson selling the Lots in the Town of Livingston.

The Grand Jury came into Court & returned a Presentment against Elizabeth Smith a widow woman who is mother of two orphan children, which children are likely to suffer it is therefore ordered that a Sci fa, Issue against the said Elizabeth Smith to shew cause why the said children should not be bound out.

Ordered that James Jenkins be appointed Constable for two years who came into Court gave security and quallified according to Law – which said Constable lives in Captain Cottons Company.

Ordered that the Grand Jury be discharged from further

Ordered that Micajah Duke, Edward Barbee, Bignal Cook, and Robert Brooks work under james Haynie overseer from Sullivans Ferry to the Fort Blount Road.
                     (Transcribed)

P 159   I John Nichols petition for a rectification of his grant of 1000 acres of land ordered by the Court that the prayer of the petitioner be granted and that the Clerk make out a Certificate of the Errors contained in said Grant and certify the same to the secretary of North Carolina.

Court Adjourns until tomorrow 8 oclock.

Friday Morning June 15th 1804 Court met according to adjournment Members
Present To wit The Worshipful   Tilman Dixon |
                                  John Lancaster & | Esquires Justices
                                  Godfrey Fowler |

John Morris by Jesse Wharton Esquire his attorney moved to set asside the
recognizance in which he was on the complaent of Nelly Gasway for Bastardy and
upon solemn argument heard as well on the part of the Plaintiff as on the part
of the Defendant the Court ordered that said Defendant be released from said
recognizance and that he be from hence discharged.

Ordered that there be a County Tax of of 12½ cents on each white poll 14 3/4
on each slave 12½ cents on each hundred acres of land, 12½ cents on each Stud
Horse 12½ cents on each Town Lot to be layed for the year 1804.

Ordered that Lee Sullivan Sheriff be appointed Collector for the State &
County tax for the year 1804 who gave Bond & security & quallified according to
Law.

Charles F. Mabias is appointed Coroner for the County of Smith for the
ensuing two years, who came into Court gave Bond with security & quallified
according to Law.

Henry Dower records his stock mark being a Staple fork in each ear and
under keel in each ear.

Court Adjourns until Court in course, to meet at the dwelling house of
William Walton Esquire.   T. Dixon J. P.
Test   S. Williams   Willis Jones J. P.
                                                 Godfrey Fowler J. P.

P 141   At a Court of Pleas and Quarter Sessions opened & hold for the County
of Smith, at the house of Colo. William Walton on Monday the 10th day of September
1804 Members Present The Worshipful   Nathaniel Brittain |
                                      John Looney and | Esquires Justices &C
                                      Godfrey Fowler |

Deed 100 Acres William Pharis to Thomas Williamson proven by the oath of
Joseph Williamson one of the subscribing witnesses thereto.

Bond 100 acres of Land William Saunders to James Condrel proven by the
oath of Samuel Comer one &f the subscribing witnesse ordered to be recorded.

Judd Strother & Henry Moore two of the Gentlemen named as Justices of the
Peace for Smith County as appears by commission from the Governor dated 4th of
August 1804 came into Court & qualified according to Law, and thereupon took
their seats.

Ordered that Abram Brittain be exempted from serving on the Venire at the
present Term.

The Commissioners who were heretofore appointed to settle with Colo. William
Martin relative to his Guardian ship over John Young, who has now arriven to full
age made report that said Martin had accounted for every he had charge of in a
satisfactory manner to said Young and that said Young & that said Young had received his negro - it is therefore ordered that said report be filed of Record.

P 142   Ordered that Elizabeth Kavanaugh, wife of Benjamin Kavanaugh Deceased, Cap. Charles Kavanaugh, & Henry Moore have letters of Administration on the Estate of said Benjamin Kavanaugh Deceased who came into Court gave Security & qualified according to Law.

Deed 3000 acres Stockley Donelson to Michael McElarath (McElrath) proven by the oath of John Looney Esquire to be the hand writing of Stockley Donelson & also to be the hand writing of the subscribing witness Ordered the same to be registered.

Ordered that Jacob Turney be appointed Constable who came into Court gave Bond & Security & qualified according to Law.

Ordered that William Turnbull, Jabez Gifford, and Abram Brittain, be appointed Patroller in Captain Daners (?) Company.

Court adjourns until Tomorrow nine oclock.

William Waltons Tuesday morning 9 oclock - Court met according to adjournment - Members Present, The Worshipful - Charles Kavanaugh ⎤
                                                James Hibits   ⎥ Esquires Justice
                                                John Looney and ⎥
                                                Abram Brittain ⎦

Ordered that Elijah Haynie be Overseer of the road in place of James Bermingham and that the same hands work under him.

Ordered that Henry Tooley be exempted from serving on the Jury a the present term.

The following persons from the Venine returned to this Term were drawn as P 143   a Grand Jury (To wit) Benjamin Johns foreman, Neil Thompson, Job Bass, James Smith, Robert Collier, Christian Boxton Daniel Mcfarland, Leonard Ballow, Edward Pharis, William Roper, Benjamin Payne, John Johnson, H. Joseph Collens, John Fite, and John Johnson Sworn & Charged.

Ordered that Jacob Turney be Constable to attend the Grand Jury who was quallified accordingly.

Ordered that Hugh McKennis be overseer of the Road from Paynes Ferry to the mouth of Paytons Creek to Alexander Pipers & that the same hands work under him as was heretofore liable to work thereon.

Deed 108 acres John Vines to Richard Rizen proven by the oath of Thomas Hall a subscribing witness.

Ordered that William Jenkins be exempted from serving on the Jury at this term.

The Inventory account account of the Estate of sales of the Estate of George Noggle Deceased is returned into Court and is ordered to be recorded.

Deed 250 acres John Williamson to William Sullivan proven by the oath of William Sullivan Junior a subscribing witness thereto.

Ordered that _____ Jarad be excused for his non attendance as a Juror at the Term he having he having given satisfactory reasons.

John L. Martin & Stephen Montgomery two of the Gentlemen named in the Commission of the Governon dated 4th August 1804 came into Court and qualified

P 144   according to law, and took their seats accordingly.

Deed 100 acres Martin Armstrong to Josiah Payne, proven by the oath of John Johnson a subscribing witness.

Deed 640 Acres John L. Martin Sheff. To Nicholass Shrum Acknowleged in open Court.

Ordered that Isaac Short be bound out as an apprentice to John Binion to learn the trade of a sadler and the said John Binion came into Court and entered into Indentures with the chairman of the Court, who bound the said apprentice accordingly.

Ordered that Tilman Dixon, William Walton, John Gordon and Michael Murphy, respectively have a Tavern License at their respective houses, who came into Court gave security according to law whereupon the Court rated as heretofore.

Ordered that David Laurence be allowed to build a saw mill on his own land on the East fork of Goose Creek provided it does not injure the land of any other person.

Ordered that the next Court be held at the late dwelling house of William Saunders Deceased and that the next adjournment be to that place.

Ordered that Elizabeth who was heretofore bound in recognizance for her appearance at this Term to shew why her children should not be bound, gave satisfactory proof that she had duly provided a comfortable substance for them or as much so as is common for a person in her situation be from hence discharged & acquitted from said charge.

Ordered that James Bradley William White, William William Pendarvis be
P 145   summoned at Livingston on the first thursday in October next to examine the materials prepared for building the Court house and report their opinion to our next Court of the value thereof.

The affidavit of Patsey Edward relative to her having a Bastard child was returned into Court by Bassel Shaw Esquire, which is filed of record.

Deed 219 acres Nathaniel Ridley to Benjamin Turner proven by the oath of Sampson Williams jone of the subscribing witnesses thereto.

Ordered that Michael Osburn be appointed Constable who came into Court gave security, But was not qualified.

The following persons were appointed to serve on the Venire to the next December Term 1804, To wit, James Bradley Isham Beasley, Jones Bishop George Bradley John Cage, William Alexander John Patterson John Douglass Senr, Charles McMurry, Abram Thompson, William Hargiss, Edward Hogan, Henry Sadler, John Lovelady, Stephen Anderson, Shadrack Moore, John Piper, Harris Bradford, James Coope, Benjamin Turner, William Wooten, William Lane, Thomas Hade, James Wallace, Samuel Casey, John Shomaker, Samuel Coruthers, William Staloup, Thomas Walker, James Wright Bignal Crook, Robert Brooks, Willie Sullivan, John Warren, John Shelton, Francis Findley, John Brevard, George Matlock & Daniel H. Burford.

Court Adjourns until Tomorrow nine oclock.

P 146   William Waltons Wednesday morning nine oclock. September 12th 1804 Court met according to adjournment. Members present, To wit, The Worshipful
James Hibbits
John Gordon Jun.
John Looney and   Esquires Justices &C.
John L. Martin

Ordered that Samuel Hannah, Isaac Wilson, James Robertson, Fredrick Skeggs, James Ray, Joseph Ray, Charles White & John Sheek be a Jury to view lay off and mark a road agreeable to law from the County line near the mouth of Wartrace crossing Cumberland River, at the mouth of Wartrace to intersect the road leading from Fort Blount to Witchers at the most convenient place and report the same to our next Court.

Ordered that John Reasonover be overseer of the Road from James Smiths, to Lancasters road near John Rights and that the same work under him as were heretofore liable to work thereon.

Deed 96 acres Stephen Montgomery to Joel Holland acknowleged in open Court.

Ordered that Willis Jones Esquires be appointed to survey a tract of land conveyed by William T. Lewis to William Sullivan Senr. being 640 acres at the mouth of Martins Creek.

Bill of Sale Joseph Collier to William Epperson proven by the oath of John Gordon Senr. a subscribing witness.

The Grand Jury came into Court and returned their Bills of Indictment, (To wit) one the State against Patrick Donoho overseer of the road & one against Lincoln Harper for an assault & Battery & one against William Porter for profane swearing & withdrew to consider of other Indictments & presentments.

P 147   The Grand Jury came into Court without making any further presentment of Indictment and being informed by the States Attorney that there was no other business to lay before them the Court discharged them.

Ordered that James Draper Esquire County Commissioner be allowed the sum of one hundred & twenty five dollars for his services in taking lists of taxable property and that he be paid out of any monies in the hands of the County Trustee not otherwise appropriated.

Mathew Harper records his stock mark, being a crop & a slit in the right ear, and a crop & under keel in the left ear.

Court adjourns until Tomorrow nine oclock.

Thursday September 13th 1804 Court met according to Adjournment Members Present (To wit) The Worshipful   John L. Martin
                                  William Marchbanks &   Esquires Justices
                                  James Roulstone

Ordered that the same Jury heretofore appointed to view lay off, & mark a road from Bowmans mill to intersect the Fort Blount road near Captain Pates be summoned to view the same & make report to our next Court.

Ordered that Isaac Scudder be appointed Constable who came into Court gave security & qualified according to law.

Ordered that Henry Moore Esquire be allowed to build a Grish & Saw Mill on Hickmans Creek upon his own land & that he be allowed the customary rates of toll for grinding.

P 148   Ordered that Robert Brooks, Bignal Creek, Edward Barber, and Micajah Duke, work under Joseph Williamson Overseer of a road.

The Inventory account of the Estate of Peter Turney Deceased is returned into Court by Sampson Williams the Executor thereof.

The Inventory account of Sales of the Estate of John Carter by Sampson Williams.

Ordered that Christian Boston be overseer of the Fort Blount Road from Michael Murphys to the top of the Ridge between Paytons & Dixons Creeks and that the following hands work under him : viz: George Thomasson, Benjamin Payne, Andrew Payne, John Thomasson, Joseph Cartwright, Edward Settles, James McFarland, Samuel Thomasson, Peter Hessian, John Sitton, Thomas Johnson, William Thompson & all those who live in them bounds work under him.

Ordered that James Kitchen Junr. be overseer of the road where Solomon Thomas was late overseer & that the same work under him as was liable to work under the late overseer.

Ordered that Elijah Haynie be Overseer of the road in place of James Bermingham the late Overseer & that the same hands work under him.

Ordered that Richard Porterfield be Overseer of the road where Henry Bohannan was late overseer and that the same hands work under him.
Test   William Marchbanks
S. Williams   John Lancaster
                                        Judd Strother
                                        Adam Dale

P 148(A)   Late Dwelling house of William Saunders Deceased Monday December 10th 1804 Court met according to Adjournment Members present (To wit)   The Worshipful   Willis Jones
                  Nathaniel Brittain | Esquires Justices
                  Godfrey Fowler and |
                  Judd Strother |

Ordered that Samuel Curothers be excepted from serving as a Juror at the Present Term. Also that William Staloup.

The following Gentlemen returned from the Venire were drawn as Grand Jurors (To wit) James Wright foreman John Piper, William Alexander, John Lovelady, Francis Findley James Bradley, John Brevard, Harris Bradford, Charles McMurry Daniel H. Burford, John Warren, Shadrick Moore, John Shelton, Willie Sullivan & Bignal Crook sworn and charged agreeable to law, withdrew to consider of Indictments & presentments & Harvey Johns a Constable sworn to attend them.

Ordered that the resignation of Lee Sullivan Esqr. Sheff. be received and that James Sullivan his duputy be appointed Sheriff in his stead until Tomorrow.

Ordered that Samuel Gott be appointed Constable who came into Court gave Security & quallified according to Law.

Ordered that John Douglass Senr. be excepted from serving at the present Term, on the Jury.

P 149   John Mungle a minor about fourteen years of age, orphan child of Daniel Mungle, came into Court, and made choice of John Brevand as his Grardian, who was approved of by the Court, being Willis Jones, Godfrey Fowler, Judd Strother.

John Patterson Records his stock mark, being a crop off both ears & an under bit & over bit in the right & an over bit in the left.

The Grand Jury returned into Court a Bill of Indictment against, James Bermingham for an assault & Battery and withdrew to consider of other presentments.

Charles F. Mabias Coroner came into Court and offered his resignation as such which received accordingly.

Ordered that James Hibits and Nathaniel Brittain settle with Daniel Alexander Administrator of the Estate of Rheubin Alexander Deceased & report to our next Court.

William Hargiss exempted from serving on the Jury at this Term for reasons appearing to the Court.

Vincient Ridley released from as an Overseer of the road and Leonard Ballow is appointed in his place, with the same hands.

Ordered that the Court Adjourn until Tomorrow nine oclock.

Tuesday December the 11th 1804 Court met according to adjournment, Members Present (To wit)   The Worshipful   James Gwin
James Draper &   Esquires Justices
Josiah Howell

Lewis Wimberly
vs   Brief
John Kennady

P 150   This day the above named Lewis Wimberly came into open Court & swore to the several matters & things contained in said Brief.

Ordered that Berryman Turner be released from serving on the Jury at this Term.

Ordered that John L. Martin Esquire late Sheff & Collector of the County of Smith be allowed a Certificate of the sum of fifteen hundred and forty six dollars & fifty four cents for insolvences for the years 1800 & 1801 for the State Tax he having made proof thereof agreeable to law.

Deed 640 acres John L. Martin Sheriff to Jacob Harvick Acknowleged in open Court.

Deed 40 Acres James Gill to Mishack Baker proven by the oath of Harris Bradford a subscribing witness.

Ordered that Gay Renolds, be allowed the sum of six hundred and fifty nine dollars & sixty one cents for the materials by him furnished, for the purpose of building a Court House in the town of Livingston and that the same be paid out of any monies in the hands of the County Trustee not otherwise appropriated.

The last Will and Testament of John Wallace Deceased was Exhibited to this Court & the Execution thereof was proven by John Wallace a subscribing witness, who also swore that he saw John McCartney subscribe the same as a witness at the same time with himself & the same is admitted to record.

Ordered that Willis Jones Esquire be allowed the sum of Eighty seven dollars for his services & other expenses incurred in running the lines of the County of Smith, & that the same be paid out of any County monies in the hands P 151 of the County Trustee not otherwise appropriated.

George Matlock Esquire is duly Elected Sheriff of Smith County who came into Court gave security & qualified according to law.

The following persons are appointed to serve on the Venire to the Superior Court, (To wit) Joel Hollard, William Walton, William Lane and Henry Tooley.

Grant Allen came into Court & resigned his appointment as Commissioner for fixing the Public buildings, and Willis Jones Esquire is appointed in his stead and thereupon the said Willis Jones, Benjamin Johns, and Wilson Cage, came into Court, gave security & qualified according to law.

The Grand Jury came into Court & returned a Bill of Indictment against Elitha Smith & Sarah Dodd for having base born children who are unprovided for and withdrew to consider of other Indictments & Presentments.

Ordered that Lee Sullivan Esquire late Sheriff be allowed the sum of sixty dollars, for his Exoficio services for nine months past and that he be paid out of any County monies in the hands of the County Trustee not otherwise appropriated.

Ordered that the next Court be held at the house of Tilman Dixon Esquire on the second Monday in March next.

The following persons were appointed to serve on the Grand and Petit Jury for the next Term, Towit, John Sanderson William Smith, James Smith, John Campbell Zachary Ford, Thomas Lancaster, Joseph Shaw, Larkin Bethel Joseph Collins, Isaac Moore, John Ward, Philip Day, Elias Johns, Jeffrey Sitton, P 152 Francis Patterson, William Payne, William Roper, David Ventress, Moses Pinkston, George Rowland, James Ballow, Thomas Draper, Andrew Greer, Randolph Wren, James Bermingham, Elijah Haynie, James Haynie, Lewis Mofarland, William Pendarvis, Henry Dancer, Hugh Stephenson Senr. William Simpson, George McWhirter, William Carter, Jeremiah Taylor, Hugh Stephenson Junior, Samuel Brittain, James Gibson, and Benjamin Barton.

On motion of John C. Hamilton Esquire, the Court ordered that John Deloach, recover Judgment against Silas Jernigan and his Securities for his faithfully performing all the duties enjoined him by law as Constable, for the sum of twenty two Dollars ninety two cents, which he the said Silas Jernigan Collected for him the said John Deloach & hath hitherto failed to account for the same Judgment is therefore awarded accordingly with cost &c.

Court Adjourns until Tomorrow nine oclock.

Wednesday December 12th 1804 Court met accordingly to adjournment.
Present the Worshipful   Willis Jones
                          Godfrey Fowler &   Esquires Justices
                          James Roulston

Deed William H. Brandon to William L. Anderson for 640 acres within the Indian Boundary proven by the oath of Richard Alexander, a subscribing witness thereto.

Deed 50 acres Zaddock Ingram to Armstreet Stubblefield proven by the oath of John Warren a subscribing witness.

P 153   Deed 10 acres James Vance to Armstreet Stubblefield proven by the oath of James Roulstone one of the subscribing witnesses.

Ordered that William Stephenson be overseer of the road in place of Stephenson resigned, & that the same hands work under him as was heretofore liable to work under, Richard Brittain who formerly was overseer of the same and that Nathaniel Brittain Esqr. furnish said Overseer with of hands.

An Inventory account of the Estate of Benjamin Kavanaugh Deceased is returned into Court by Henry Moore Esquire one of the Administrators & is ordered to be recorded.

Deed 340 Acres Robert Hargis to William Williams Proven by the oath of

Mathew Milton, a subscribing witness.

Deed _____ David Looney To Jeremiah Taylor proven by the oath John Sullivan a subscribing witness thereto.

Deed 30 Acres Benjamin Wootton to David Hodges Proven by the oath of William Wootton a subscribing witness thereto.

Deed _____ Peter Lemmons to Thomas Graves proven by the oath of Thomas Graves a subscribing witness thereto.

Deed 40 acres Amos Freeman To Jeremiah Taylor Proven by the oath of John Sullivan a Subscribing witness.

Deed 230 acres Zachariah Wilson to Christian Boston proven by the oath of Jesse Wharton a subscribing witness.

Deed 240 acres David King to John Jones proven by the oath of William Turnbull a subscribing witness thereto.

Deed 40 acres John Gill to Mishack proven by the oath Harris Bradford.

Court adjourns until Tomorrow morning Eight oclock.

P 154   Thursday morning December 13th 1804 Court met according to Adjournment Members Present, (To wit) The Worshipful   James Gwin
                                                Basel Shaw
                                                Willis Jones   } Esquires Justices
                                                William Gregory &
                                                Godfrey Fowler

John Gordon Esquire came into Court & took the oath of Deputy Sheriff, the oath to Support the Constitution of the United States and the State of Tennessee.

The Grand Jury came into Court, & returned two Bills of Indictment against William Woodford and three presentments :viz: one against John Jones, one against William and one against Samuel Young and withdrew to consider of other presentments & Indictments.

Deed 10 Acres James Saunders Executor of William Saunders Deceased to Garrol Wright Acknowleged in open Court.

Deed 100 acres Richard Brittain to Robert McNeeley Acknowleged in open Court.

Charles F. Mabias who is Elected Coroner came into Court & refused to act, or to enter into bond & security and withdrew.

Samuel Young was brought into Court and fined in the sum of twenty dollars for a contempt offered this Court - and ordered into the custody of David Rorex, a Constable for an hour & a half.

P 155   Ordered that Randolph Wren be fined the sum of twenty dollars for a contempt offered this Court & on motion of the said Randolph Wren the fine levied as aforesaid was mitigated to three dollars & costs, Judgment accordingly.

Deed 220 acres Thomas Hickman to James Gwin proven by the oath of Willis Jones, Esquire a subscribing witness.

Deed 420 acres Thomas Hickman to Thomas Wilkerson Proven by the oath of

Willis Jones Equire a subscribing witness.

Deed 140 acres John Gwin to David Jennings proven by the oath of James
Gwin Esquire a subscribing witness thereto.

Deed _____ acres John Gwin to Doctor Jennings proven by the oath of
James Gwin Esquire a subscribing witness thereto.

Deed 100 acres James Saunders Executor and Nancy Saunders Executrix to
Andrew Hibbits proven by the oath of James Hibits a subscribing witness thereto.

Ordered that Thomas Jones be overseer of the road where Willis Jones
Esquire was late Overseer and that all the hands living on fall creek & rack-
coon branch work under him also all the hands who were heretofore liable to
work thereon.

Ordered that Lewis Corder be Overseer of the road where Lewis Mcfarland
was late overseer, and that the same hands work under him.

Ordered that Jacob Dice be overseer of the road in place of Thomas Banks
late overseer & that the same hands work thereon.

Ordered that Sampson William be overseer of that part of the road where
Michael Murphy was late overseer and that Archibald Sleane Esquire furnish said
Overseer with a list of hands.

Ordered that Joseph Sullivan be overseer of the road where Daniel Alexander
was late Overseer - that the same work under him who worked thereon before.

P 156   The Grand Jury came into Court and returned a Bill of Indictment
against Andrew Anderson and one against James Cunningham and on motion of their
foreman to be discharged and being informed by the County Solicitor that there
was no other business to lay before them The Court ordered that they be discharged and they are accordingly discharged.

The Petition of John Bradley was filed to close the lines of a tract of
land, of Maj. Thomas Donoho's on Goose Creek and John L. Martin is appointed
surveyor to close the same.

John Gordon exhibited his stock mark being two Swallow Forks and an
under bit in the right ear ordered to be recorded.

Ordered that the fine heretofore levied on Samuel Young for a contempt
offered this Court be mitegated to one dollar and twenty five cents & cost.

Ordered that the part of the road where William Turnbull is Overseer
be divided between said Turnbull and Samuel Coruthers former Overseer of said
road. that is to say Samuel Coruthers to work from the fork near his still
house to the ford of the East fork of Goose Creek near Brevards and that
william Turnbull work from there to Jabez Giffords and that Nathaniel Brittain
& James Hibbits furnish them with a list of hands.

Friday Morning December 14th 1804 Court met according to adjournment
Present the Worshipful.   John L. Martin ⎤
                          Godfrey Fowler & ⎬   Esquires Justices &C.
                          James Cotton   ⎦

Ordered that Godfrey Fowler be Guardian to Sally Payne who came into Court
& entered into Bond and Security in presence John Lancaster John L. Martin &
Jas. Cotten Esquires.

P 157   Ordered that the Inventory account of the Estate of James Rowland Deceased returned into Court by Robert Rowland the administrator be received & ordered to be recorded.

Ordered that Willis Jones be appointed, by consent of parties, to survey the Lands in dispute between Robert Slothart & George Smith and that he return three Just & fair <u>planns</u> thereof to our next County Court.

Court Adjourns until Tomorrow nine oclock.

Saturday December 15, 1804 Court met according to adjournment Members Present (To wit) The Worshipful   James Hibbits

John L. Martin &   Esquires Justices

Nathaniel Brittain

Court Adjourns until the second Monday in March next, to meet at the dwelling house of Tilman Dixon.

James Hibbits

Test   Sampson Williams   John L. Martin

Nathaniel Brittain.

(This book skips from the last date of 1804 to 1835.)

P 158   Tuesday morning the 24 of December 1835 Court meet according to adjournment Present Samuel D. MoMy. (McMurry
              Hny. B. McDonald
              Exum Whity (Whitley) and
              Marthias West Esqr.

The Commissioners appointed to lay off and set apart a years provision to the
widow and famly (family) of Moses Schoot Dec. made their report to Court, and the
motion ordered to be recorded.

On motion and petition It is ordered by the Court that Solomon Debow, Alfred
A. Brevard Cyrus W. Brevard, Joseph Gifford and Ephraim Pursly be appointed Commissioners to divide the Negros belonging to the Estate of Moses Scott dec. between
the distributees of said Estate and make report to next Court.

Ordered that O. B. Hubbard and Andrew Allison be appointed Commissioners } VOID
to settle with the Clerk of Smith County from the year 1835.

Orderéd that Harry Hogg and Wm. Hart be appointed Commissioners to settle } VOID
with David (?) K. Timberlake Trustee for Smith County for the year 1835.

Ordered that John G. Park and William Owen be appointed Commissioners to } VOID
settle with Samuel P. Harvard Shff. of Smith County for the year 1835.

The Commissioners appointed to settle with John Bradly Ex. of the Estate of
Daid (David) Cochran Dec. made their report to Court which was received and ordered
to be recorded.

Ordered that John Shelton pay a single Tax on 360 acres of land and 8 Black
Poles which amounted to nine dollars and ten cents, and was paid for said Shelton
by Solomon Debow Esqr.

On motion ordered that Miles West be appointed administrator of the Estate of
Jesse West Jr. Dec. who came into Court and qualified together with David Hogg his
security and into in the sum of six thousand dollars conditioned as the law directs
Letters of administration is granted him of said ded. Estate.

P 159   The administrators of the Estate of Moses Scott ded. rendered into Court
as Inventory of said ded. Estate, and on motion ordered to be rederded.

The administrator of Archd. Cannon ded. reports that no property belong to
the ad. ded. has come into his hands.

Proclamation having been made the Court procoeded to the election of a Clerk
for the Court of Pleas and quarter sessions for the County of Smith, and to that
office did elect John J. Burnett who came into Court and was duly qualified as directed by law & together with his securites Jonah Mosses Spencer Kelly Samuel P.
Harvard and Swan Thompson and entered into bond as follows to wit, Know all men by
these that we John J. Burnett, Josiah Moses Spencer Kelly Samuel P. Harvard and
Swant Thompson all of Smith County and State of Tennessee are held and firmly bound
unte Newton Cannon Governor and his sucssors in office in the sum of five thousand
dollars to which payment well and truly to be made and done we bind ourselves our
heirs Executors and administrators and assignes Jointly and severally firmly by
these presents sealed with our seals ad dated this 24 day of November 1835.

The condition of the above obligation is such that whereas the above bond John
J. Burnett has this day been duly elected Clerk of the Court of Pleas and quarter
Sessions for said County of Smith now if the said John J. Burnett shall well and truly

keep all the record of said Court and shall faithfully and truly perform according
to law during his continuanse in the office aforesaid then this obligation to be
void, else remain in full force and virtue John J. Burnett (seal) Josiah Moses (Seal)
Samuel P. Harvard (Seal) Swan Thompson (Seal)

Know all men by these presents that we John J. Burnett Josiah Mosses, Spencer
Kelly, Saml. P. Harvard and Swan Thompson of Smith County and State of Tennessee,
an held and filing bond into Henry B. McDonald Esqr. Chairman of Smith County County
and his sucssors in office in the sum of one thousand dollars to which payment well
P 160 and truly to be made, we bind Ourselves Our heirs Executors administrators
and assignes Jointly and Severally firmly by these presents sealed with our seals
and dated this 24 day of November 1835.

The condition of the above abligation is such that whereas John J. Burnett
has this day been appointed Clerk of the Court of Pleas and quarter sessions for
the Couty of Smith now if the said John J. Burnett shall well and truly pay one
all fines and forfeitures or all moves that may come to his hands for the use of
the County to the County Trustee or any other person or persons legally authorized
to rev. the same or any monies that may come to his hands for the use of others by
virtue of his office aforesaid, to them their agents or attorneys lawfully authorized
to be void or else remain in full force and virtue signed sealed and acknowleged in
the presence of us, John J. Burnett (Seal) Josiah Moses (Seal) Spencer Kelly (Seal)
Saml. P. Harvand (Seal) Swan Thompson (Seal).

Barkley Kyle vs William Floyd, Garnishments Came the plaintiff by his attorney
and the defendant in proper person, and the said defendant being examined on oath
answers and says that he had in his possession at the time of the service of the
Garnishment upon him in this cause to wit on 24th Nov. 1835 "one feather bed Rapt
up in a bed cord, one barrel and one box containing articles unknown to said Floyd
but supposed by him to contain articles of queens ware &C belonging to John P.
Williams. It is therefore considered by the Court that said property be delivered
up by said Floyd to the Sheriff of Smith County and by him sold to satisfy the
plaintiffs debt, interest and cost and the cost of this Garnishment.

The administrators of the Estate of (name omitted) rendered into Court an
Inventory and act. of sales of sd. doeasd. Estate and on motion ordered to be recorded.

Ordered by the Court that Simon P. Hughes be appointed Guardian for Lucian B.
Horace M. Herbert H. and Octavia D. Sullivan deod. and entered into bond in the sum
P 161 of six thousand dollars together with John Bransford and David A. Mc-
Cachin(?) his secretary approved by the Court.

William B. Pursley is appointed Guardian to Harvick Jones Pursley a minor within
the age of twenty one years, who came into Court and qualified, and together with
Isaac Goodall and Solomon Debow his securities, intered into bond in the sum of five
thousand dollars conditioned as the law directs.

John R. Daugherty |
     vs | Garnishments - Came the Plaintiff by his attorney and the
Moses Robinson | defendant in proper person and the said defendant being
duly sworn as Garnishee in this cause and says that he had no goods and effects in
his hands on possession at the time of the service of the garnishment in this cause
Belonging to Archie Robinson in this cause That he bought from said Archer Robinson
in August last four hundred acres of land it being the tract of land on which the
late Steven Robinson deod. for which he gave the said Archie one hundred and fifty
dollars in cash and executed to him his note for four hundred and fifty dollars at
four years after date. that said tract of land is subject to the dower of the widow
of Stephen Robinson deod. one hundred and fifty acres being subject to said widow
for her dower to be laid off out of such part as she may choose. He further says
that he does not know whether the said Archer has transferred said note of $450
nor does he owe said Archer anything besides said note nor does he know of any other

person or persons who has any of the goods and effects of the Archer in their
hands or that owe him anything, whereupon on om motion It is considered by the
Court that said Moses Robinson be discharged from the garnishment in this cause
and that recover against the plaintiff his costs by him about his defence in this
behalf expended.

Garland McCollister is excused from further attendance as a Juror at this term.

p 162   The executrix of the last will and testament of Thompson Atwood rendered
into Court an Inventory of the said ded. Estate, which on motion is ordered to be
recorded.

The administrator of the Estate of Risen Roland ded. rendered into Court an
Inventory and aćt. of sales of said deed. Estate which is ordered to be recorded.

James Shelton adm. |
        vs | Debt - This cause is contd. on the affidavit of the
Majr. A. Beasley | Debt, and on motion a commission is award him to take
the Deposition of James Culbreath of Tipton County in this state, by giving the
plaintiff fifteen days notice of the term and place of taking the same.

The commissioners appointed to divide and make partition of a certain tract
of land belong to Jno. B. Armstrong & Mary A. E. McCall made their report to Court
which is ordered to be recorded.

On motion present Esquire Hogg,   Winfree,
                   McDonald,   West,
                   Goodall,   Evans,
                   Debow,   Coffee,
                   Mosses,   Thompson,
                   Whitley,   Goodner and
                                       McCrary who voted in the affirmative.
It is ordered by the Court that the County Trustee pay to the following sums of
money for the following purposes, out of any money in his hand not otherwise appropriated to wit. To Hubbard Owents & Co.
    For 2 padlocks 4 staples & 2 Hasps finished for the Court House Gate - $2.25;
    To Thomas Wooten for sledge Hammer & Crowbar - 8.55.

P 163   The following Justices being present and all voting in the affirmative,
to wit, Messers McDonald,   West,
                Hogg,   Evans,
                Goodall,   Coffee,
                Debow,   Thompson,
                Moses,   Goodner &
                Whitley,   Saml. D. McMurry it is ordered that the County
                Winfree,   Trustee pay the following bills of cost certified
from the Circuit Court, to wit, State vs Jno. Waters -
    Clk. Harts fees pr. transcript-------------------$ 9.31½
    No. 8 Atts Gen Yerger two fees   2.50
    Shff. Howard fees   2.16½
    Witness Joseph Hales   6.62½
    Saml. Ayres   6.12½
    Tho. J. Tyree   2.75
    Tho. T. Tyree   7.50
                                                       ──────
                                                               36.95
    State vs Tho. Ferrell Clk Hart   do   do   do   7.62½
    Atts Gen Yerger   2.50
    Shff Howard   2.00
                                                       ──────
                                                               12.12½

State vs A. Hallum Clk Harts   do   do   do   6.81½
Atts Gen Yerger   2.50
Shff. Howard   1.54
                                             10.53

State vs D. Hornbeck Clk Hart   do   do   do   7.62½
atts Gen Yerger   2.50
Shff. Howard   1.66
                                             11.78

State vs D. C. Dixon Clk Hart   do   do   do   6.50
Atts Genl. Yerger   2.50
Shff. Howard   1.41½
   "   Lauderdale   .12½
                                             10.53

State vs R. Rison Clk Hart   .do   do   do   5.65
Atts Gen. Yerger   2.50
Shff. Howard,   1.79
   "   Lauderdale   .12½
                    No.   10.06½
State vs J. W. Moore 12 Clk Hart do   do   do   6.15
Atts Gen. Yerger   do   do   do   2.50
Shff. Howard   do   do   do   1.54
                    No.   10.19
State vs J. W. Moore 13 Clk Hart   do   do   do   7.06
Atts Gen. Yerger   2.50
Shff. Howard   1.54
                    No.   11.10
State vs J. W. Moore 14 Clk Hart do   do   do   8.35
Stts Gen. Yerger   2.50
Shff. Howard   1.54
                                           12.29

State v B. Cardwell Clk Hart   do   do   do   6.37
Atts. Gen Yerger   2.50
Shff. Howard   1.29
Shff. Lauderdale   .12½
                                           10.28½

State vs B. Rowland Clk Hart   do   do   do   6.87
Atts Gen Yerger   2.50
Shff Howard   .29
Shff Payne   1.00
                                           10.66

State vs J. Bates Clk Hart   do   do   do   6.16
Atts Gen Yerger   2.50
Shff Howard   2.29
                                           10.85

State v J. Killoughty(?) Clk Hart do   do   do   6.06
Atts Gen Yerger   2.50
Shff Howard   2.29
                                           10.85

State v M. Minick(?) Clk Hart do   do   do   3.81½
Atts Gen Yerger   2.50
Shff Howard   .50
                                         6.81½

State v J. J. Hardwick Clk Hart   do   do   do   4.50
Atts Gen pro tem Hubbard   2.50
Shff. Howard   .54
                                         7.54

State v S. Clements Clk Hart   do   do   do   4.50
Atts Gen pro tem Hubbard   2.50
Shff Howard   .54
                                         7.54

State v W. Hickman Clk Hart do	do	do	5.68 3/4		
Atts Gen Yerger			2.50		
Shff Harvard			1.62½		
Shff Lauderdale			.12½		
				9.93 3/4	
State v W. Sanders Shff Howard			.50		
Witness W. Ragland			3.00		
Wm. D. Wright			3.00		
				6.50	
State vs W. Whitley Shff Howard			.25		
State Waters 9(?) Shff Howard			1.00		
				$208.11	

P 164   Elijah Haile
         to   Continue - A deed of conveyance from Elijah Haile to
    Robert Burton   Robert Burton, bearing date the 22d day of August, 1835,
for a tract of land lying in Smith County, on the south side of Cumberland river,
near Knob Spring and containing forty two acres more or less, was produced for pro-
bate in open Court, and thereupon the said bargainor Elijah Haile, who is personally
know to the Court in open Court acknowleged that he executed said deed for the pur-
poses therein contained, and the same is ordered to be certified for Registration.

Upon motion & the following Justices being in Court, and all voting in the
affirmative, it is ordered that the following claims be paid by the County Trustee,
to wit, Messrs. McDonald,   Winfree,
                 Hogg,   Evans,
                 Goodall,   Coffee,
                 Debow,   Thompson,
                 Moses,   Goodner and
                 Whitley,   S. D. McMry.

The State
      vs   Jailer Alexander a/cs filed $35 .50
A. Rowland

State
      vs   Kyler a/cs filed part allowed $ 4.00;
Gillispie

Jailer Alexander a/cs filed	4.37½
Edward Mitchells a/c for crobar, sledge & 2 small Hammers	8.95
Shff Howard a/cs for wood & candles for Court, to this date	19.25
Clerk Picketts a/cs for making out Tax list	25.00
" transcript of list for measurer	2.50
" Ex officio services	50.00
	$77 .50

Att. Gen. Yerger for Ex officio services 50.00 and it is further ordered by
the Court that the Clerk of this Court issue certificates on the Roll of Jurors
Certificate from the Circuit Court at October Term 1835 and that the County trustee
pay said certificates in the same measure as Jurors of the original venire, it
appearing to the satisfactions of the Court that said jurors were summoned by the
Sheriff and detained at said Circuit Court to await the election of Jurors in State
trials pending therein and that they had been generally summoned at their homes and
not from among the immediate bystanders.

P 165   Order that Parks Chandler be appointed overseer of the road from William
Carter to Travis(?) Finly(?) and that part of the road leading to James Owens and
have the same hands and bounds.

The Sheriff returned the Venire faceas to this term from which the following

Gentlemen good and lawfull men for said County were elected a Jury of Grand inquest for the body of this County to wit, Judd Strother, foreman, Luis(?) P. Hicks, Ned Read, Henry Williams Wammock Parker Taylor Atchley Robert Kenny John Reeves Solomon McMry.(McMurry) James A. Scruggs, Josiah Davidson, Zadock B. Roberts William Shoemake who were duly sworn and charged by Atts General for the State returned to Consabl. for their punishment &C.

John Sampson Constable sworn to attend the Grand Jury at this Term.

Court adjourned until tomorrow morning 10 oclock.

Henry B. McDonald
S. D. McMurry
Exum Whitley

P 166   Wednesday morning Court meet present(pursuant) to adjournment Present Esqr. McDonald
McMy. (McMurry) and
Whitley.

Thomas B. Oakly |
To | Deed of Conveyance for 34½ acres of land from Thomas B.
Isaac Miller | Oakley to Isaac Miller lying in Smith County & bearing date 15(Nov) (or March) 1835 was produced in open Court, and was duly proven by the oaths of D. A. McEachin and Jonathan S. Fox(?) the subscribing witnesses thereto and on motion ordered to be certified for Registration.

The State |
vs | Int. A. B. (?) -   This day came the solicitor Genl.
Wilson Boulton | for the state and the Deft in proper person, and the Deft. beca use he will not contend says he is guilty as charged in the Bill of Indictment and puts himself upon the mercy of the Court. It is therefore considered by the Court that the defendant pay a fine of two dollars and the cost of this prosecution Alexander James herein open Court acknowleged himself. security for the payment of fine and cost. and that Execution may issue against him together with the defendant for the same.

P 167   The State |
vs | Inst. A. B. -   This day came the solicitor General
John Waters | for the state, and the defendant. in pasper person and being charged upon the Bill of Indictment plead not guilty thereto and for his trial puts himself the cost then the attorney general doeth the like and thereupon came a Jury of good and lawfull men to wit, Champ Thomas, Edwan Evans, Lemuel(?) Tuny(Turney), Johathan Fuston, Gregory Moore, William Reeves, Winston Candler(?) Horace Oliver, Stirling Jackson, Moses Reeves and Andrew W. Jouvaneau and Caleb Read, who being elected twice and sworn the truth to speak upon the issue joins upon this oath do say that the defendant is not guilty in manner and form as charged in the bill of Indictment. It is therefore considered by the Court that the defendant be discharged from this prosecution and that the cost of this prosecution be taxed for the inspection of the Court.

State |
vs | Presamt. Affray -   This day came the solicitor general
L. B. Turner | for the state and the defendant in proper person and the defendant because he will not contend says he is guilty as charged in as charged and put himself upon the mercy of the Court. It is therefore considered by the Court that the deft. pay a fine of two dollars and fifty cents and the cost of this prosecution Thomas T. Tyree here in open Court acknowlege himself security for the payment of fine and cost and that execution may issue against him together with the defendant for the same.

P 168   The State |
vs | Presamt. vs Road
James Evits |

This day came the solicitor general for the state and the deft. in proper personand says he will not contend because he is guilty as charged in the present- ment and puts himself upon the Mercy of the Court. It is therefore considered thatthe deft. pay a fine of two dollars and fifty cents and cost of this prosecution Andrew Payne here in open Court acknowleged himself security for the payment of fine & cost and that Exegution may issue against him together with the deft for the same.

P 169   State
           vs   Presentment Affray - This day came the solicitor
     Spthaner(?) Colby   general for the state. and the defendant in proper person and says he will not contend because he is guilty as charged in this pro- secution and puts himself upon the mercy of the court. It is therefore considered by the Court that the defendant pay a fine of two dollars and fifty cents, the co of this prosecution. John Colley has in open Court acknowleged himself security for the payment of fine and cost and that execution may issue against him together with the deft. for the same.

     State
       vs   Presmt. Gaming - This cause is contind. by consent and
  Henry H. Jones   Robert Allen Jr. acknowledges himself indebted to the State of Tennessee in the sum of two hundred and fifty dollars for the use of the state to be void on condition that the said Henry H. Jones make his personal appearance before this Court at the next term to be held for the county of Smith at the court house in Carthage on the first Wednesday after the 4th Monday in February next to answer the state an a presentment for gaming and not depart without the leave of said court first had and obtained or otherwise being legally disdharged.

    State of Tennessee
        vs   Gaming - Came the attorney General who prosecutes
  John Waters   for the State and Buckner S. Cardwell who had been regularly summoned as a witness for the state in this cause, being solemnly called, came not but made default. It is therefore considered by the Court that the state of Tennessee recover against the said Buckner S. Cardwell the sum of two hundred and fifty dollars. the amount of the forfeiture in the subpoena mentioned unless he shall shall attend at the next term of this and show his inability to attend and give evidence in the above cause as he was this day bound to do & that sceias faceas issue to make known &C.

P 170   State of Tennessee
           vs   Gaming - Came the attorney General who prosicuted
     Bird Read   for the state, and Buckner S. Cardwell who has been regularly summoned as a witness on the part of the State in this cause, being solemnly called came not but made default. It is therefore considered by the Court that the state of Tennessee recover against the said Buckner S. Cardwell the sum of two hundred and fifty dollars the amt. of the forfeiture mentioned in said subpoena unless the said Buckner S. shall shew at the next term of this court his inability to attend at the present term and give evidence in the cause as by said subpoena he was this day bound to do and that Sci. Fa. issue to make known &c And with the assent of Court the attorney General enters a noli Prase Que as to the said Bird Read in this cause.

    State
      vs
  James McCreely (or McKiney?)   On motion of the atto Gen it is (unreadable) that a pls caps to Jackson and Smith Counties.

    State
      vs
  John Hastny   On motion of the atto genl. it is ordered by the court a at (?) caps issue.

State
vs
Allno. James (Jones?)

On motion of the atto genl. It is ordered by the
Court that a notice prosiqu. presented(?).

Thomas Leach is appointed administrator of the estate of Coleman Leach ded.
who came into Court and qualified together with his security George C. Gifford his
security and enter into bond in the sum of six hundred dollars conditioned as the
law directs. Letters of administration is granted on said ded. estate.

P 171   Jacob H. Buton is appointed administrator of the estate of May Burton
ded. who came into Court and qualified together with his securities William Carter
and Franklin White in the sum of two thousand five hundred dollars conditioned as
the law directs. Letters of administration is granted.

State
vs
Thomas A. Gillispie

Peau Recognizance - Came the attorney General who
prosecutes for the state and the defendant in proper
person. the the prosecutors failing to appear and rebind the defendant, It is
considered by the Court that said Defendant be discharged from this recognizance.

State
vs
Robert Bowman

Gaming - Came the attorney General and says he no further
intends prosecuting the defendant in this cause and with
the assent of the Court a noti prase qui is entered in this cause, against the
defendant. It is therefore considered by the the the Court that a noti prase qui be
and the sum is hereby entered and It appearing to the satisfaction of the Court
that Buckner S. Cardwell a witness for the state in this cause had been regularly
summoned by the sheriff of this County, and being solemnly called came not but
made default. It is therefore considered by the Court that the state of Tennessee
recover against the said Buckner S. Cardwell the sum of two hundred and fifty dollars
the amt. of the forfeiture in the subpoena mentioned unless he shall show to this
Court at the next term his inability to attend at the present term and Give (unresmable
in this cause as he was at this term bound to do and that a Sci Fa issue to make
known &C.

P 172   John McMurry
vs
Full Hughad

Motion - Came the by their attorney and the plaintiff
dismisses his Full Hughad the defendant here in open Court assume the payment of the
cost. It is therefore considered by the court that the plaintf. man vs the deft.
the cost of this motion.

On Petition and motion. It is ordered by the Court that Jacob H. Burton
adm. of the Estate of Max Burton ded. sell two negro slaves Judy and Ben belong
to said Estate. in a credit of six months at such betw   this and the next
Court as the said administrator may think proper, by taking bond and good. security
for the purchase money and make report to next Court.

On motion of atto Genl. and It appearing to the satisfaction of the Court
that Buckner S. Cardwell a witness for and in behalf of the state of Tennessee vs
John Waters. presentment gaming, which cause is now called and set for trial. that
the said Buckner S. Cardwell had been duly subponead as appears from the return
of the Sheriff of Smith County he failing to appear though solemnly called but made
default. It is therefore considered by the Court that the state of Tennessee two
hundred and fifty dollars. The forfeiture mentioned in said subponea against the
P 173   Buckner S. Cardwell for his non attendance unless he the said Buckner S.
Cardwell show to the satisfaction of this Court at the next term his inability to
attend on this day and give evidence in this cause as he was this day bound to and
that secifa issue today bound to & make known.

State
vs   This day came the atto. Genl. for the state of Tennessee and
John Waters   says he no further intends to prosecute the deft. and by per-
mission of the Court It is ordered that a Prasequi be entered.

State
vs   Presentment neusiance - This day came the attorney
Robert D. Hoover   Gentl. for the state and the defendant and a Jury of
Good and lawful men to wit Champe.

P 174   State
vs   Presentment Nusions - This day came the atto. Genl. for
R. D. Hoover   the State and the deft. in Proper Person and being Arraigned for this presentment and pleads not guilty thereto and for his Trial puts
himself upon his County and the At. Genl. doth the like. Then came a Jury of good
and lawful men to wit. C. Thomas Edward Evans Sal. (Samuel) Turney Jonathan Fuston
Gregory Moore William Reeves Winston Chandler, Stirling Jackson Moses Reeves and
W. Jouvanceau Hardy Jones and Mathew Nichols who being elevted true. and sworn the
truth to speak upon the issue Joined and after hearing a part of the Testimony in
this cause and because this cause cannot be ended on this day. The Jurors afd. are
permitted to dispense until morrow morning 10 oclock.

State
vs   Contend until tomorrow John S. Brown (?) is appointed atto.
John Stafford   Geo.pro tem for the present term of this Court who took the
oath prescribed by law.

P 175   Court adjourned until tomorrow morning 10 oclock.

                                           Exum Whitley
                                           Henry B. McDonald
                                           S. D. McMurry

Thurdday morning Court meet pursuant to adjournment Present Esqr. McDonald,
                                                           McMurry, and
                                                           Whitley

On motion Samuel D. McMurry Esqr. is appointed administrator of the Estate
of William Smith ded. who came into Court and qualified together with Brick F.
Martin his security and entered into bond in the sum of three hundred dollars conditioned as the law directs. Letters of administration is granted him on said
ded. Estate.

The administrator of the Estate of Elisha Bins(?) ded. rendered into Court
and inventory and acct. of sales and on motion ordered to be recorded.

State
vs   Inst. A. & B. - This cause is contend. in affidavit of the
John Stafford   att. General. The grand Jury came into Court and made presentment against Lee Squires overseer of the Road ordered that a capescis issue
vs the defendant.

The Grand Jury came into Court and present a Bill of Indictment A. B. against
William F. McDonald on motion it is ordered that a capias issue against the defendant.

P 176   On motion It is ordered by the Court that Elijah Toney pay a single Tax
on two hundred and thirty four acres of (and?) land, 2 Black Poles and 5 1/3 Town
Lots for the years 1834 and 1835 amounting to fourteen dollars, which amount is
paid by O. B. Hubbard agent for said Tony. paid.

On motion ordered that Toney & Caplinger pay a single Tax on two hundred and fifty four acres of deeded land for 1834 & 5 which is paid by O. B. Hubbard $254 paid.

On motion ordered that Tony Baily & Co. pay a single Tax on one half town lot for the years 1834 & 5. 89 cents paid.

Robert Doubty(?) }
vs } Garnishments - Came the parties by their attornies and
James Coruthers } The motion of the Defendant to quash the proceedings in
this cause is overrulled and on motion of the plaintiff by his attorney a scrivi facias is awarded him to make known to defendant that he appear at the next term of this Court & show cause if any he can why the Judgment after Justice of the peace in this cause should not be revived against him to all which the defendant by his counsel excepts.

P 177   State of Missouri County of Calloway Set. I. Irvine O. Hackaday Clerk of the County Court within and for the County aforesaid do certify that at a County Court (it being a Court of Record) called and specifically held for Callaway County at the Court house in the Town of Fulton in said County of Calloway. On Monday the fifteenth day of June A.D. 1835 Lucy Ann Parker, Elizabeth Carolin Parker and Peter Francis Parker infant orphans of Fannie Parker ded, over the age of fourten years, appeared in Court and made choice of thier Grand Father Jeffry Litton(?) for their Guardian and thereupon he the said Jeffry Litton was by said Court duly appointed Guardian for the infant orphans aforesaid, and entered into and Executed Bond for the faithfull discharge of his duties as Guardian aforesaid in the penalty of two thousand five hundred dollars with Exra B. Litton and James Tate his securities who were approved of by said Court conditioned as the law directs.

P 178   The State }
vs } This day came again the atto. Genl. for the state and
R. D. Hoover } the Deft. in proper person and also a Jury of Good and
lawful men to wit Champ T. Thomas Edward Evans, Leml. Turney Jonathan Fuston Gregory Moore Wm. Reeves, Winston Candler Stirling Jackson, Moses Reeves, Andrew W. Jouvanceau, Hardy Jones & Mathew Nichols who were the same Jury elected tried and sworn. and after sometime spent in hearing Testimony and the argument of Consel because it seems to the Court that the trial of this cause cannot be concluded this day by consent of the parties with the assent of the Court, the Jurors are permitted to dispanse and meet again tomorrow 10 oclock. A 1g. (?)

Court adjourns until tomorrow morning 10 oclock.

S. D. McMurry
Exum Whitley
Don C. Dixon.

P 179   Friday morning Court meet pursuant to adjournmt. Present Esqr. McDonald
Whitley and
McMurry.

On motion ordered that John Kelly vs John Lancaster Esqr. and Stephen Robinson are appointed Commissioners to settle with Spencer Kelly admr. of James Shepherd dc. and report to next Court.

The administrator of the Estate of Nathaniel Cody dc. rendered into Court an Inventory a partial act. of sales of said Estate and on motion ordered to be recorded.

Hardy Jones a Juror at this Term proved 3 days attendance and 2 feriages State vs Hoover.

The Grand Jury came into Court and made presentments for Dan C. Dixon for Gaming ordered that a capias issue.

The Grand Jury came into Court and made presentment against William Calhoon for Gaming ordered that a capias issue.

The Grand Jury came into Court and made presentment against Bird Read for gaming ordered that a capias issue.

P 180   The Grand Jury came into Court and made presentment against Jesse Powell for an indictment for an assault and Battery ordered that a capias issue.

The grand Jury came into Court and made presentment against Daniel A. Mc-Eachern Paschal W. Brian presentment an affray ordered that a capias issue.

A record forming the appointment of Feffrey Sutton Guardian to Lucy Ann Parker, Elizabeth Carolin Parker and Peter Francis Parker infant orphans of Francis Parker decd. from the County Court of Callaway County in the state of Missouri under seal of said Court with the certificate thereto appointed was this day produced in open Court and on motion, ordered to be recorded.

John P. Williams
    To   Deed for 71 Acres of land from John P. Williams to John
John Moore   Moore bearing date the 22nd day of February 1830 was this day produced in open Court and the due execution thereof by the bargainor was duly proven by the oaths of George W. Reasonover and John Dundan two of the subscribing witnesses thereto and on motion the same is ordered to be certified for Registration.

P 181   Isaac Moore & W. A. Moore
    To   Deed for 30 acres of land lying in Smith
John P. Williams   County on the waters of Hickmans Creek bearing date the 20 day of February 1830 was in open Court produced and duly proven in open Court by the oaths of A. Robinson and John Moore, the subscribing witnesses thereto, and on motion ordered to be certified for Registration.

The State
    vs   Presentment Gaming - This day came the attorney General
Theodore Ferrill   for the state and the defendant in proper person and say he will not contend, because he is guilty as charged in the presentment and puts himself upon the mercy of the Court. It is therefore considered by the Court that the defendant pay a fine of ten dollars and the cost of this prosecution. It is further ordered that he be put into the custody of the Sheriff until he give security for the payment of fine and cost or discharge the same.

P 182   The State
    vs   Indictment Neusiance - This day came the attorney
Robert D. Hoover   General for the state and the defendant in proper person and Then came the same Jury that was elected tried & sworn in this cause on Wednesday last upon their oaths do say that the defendant is not guilty as charged in the presentment. It is thereupon considered by the Court that the deft. be discharged.

The State of Tennessee
    vs   Indictment for Assault & Battery Came here in open
William F. McDonald   Court Willis Coggin and acknowledges himself indebted to the state of Tennesse e in the sum of two hundred and fifty dollars to be levied off his goods & chattels Lands and tenements for the use of the state to be void on condition that he make his personal appearance before the Court of Pleas and quarter sessions next to be held for the County of Smith at the Court house in Carthage on the first Wednesday after the fourth Monday in February next to prosecute and give evidence in behalf of the state against the said Defendant William F. McDonald on the above charged and not depart without being legally discharged.

P 183   The State of Tennessee
                    vs   Came here in
          James Jones, Bird Read, Don C. Dixon & William Calhoun   open Court
Braxton M. Key and acknowledges himself indebted to the state of Tennessee in the
sum of two hundred and fifty dollars in each of the above cases to be levied of his
goods and chattels lands and tenements for the use of the state that is to say two
hundred and fifty dollars in the case of the state against James Jones. Two hundred
and fifty dollars in the case of the state against Bird Read. Two hundred and fifty
dollars in the case of the state against Don C. Dixon and Two hundred and fifty
dollars in the case of the state against William Calhoun to be void on condition
that the said Braxton McKey make his personal at the next term of this court to be
held for the county of Smith at the Court house in Carthage in Carthage on the first
Wednesday after the fourth Monday in February next to give evidence in behalf of
the state against the above named defendants on the above charge of unlawful gaming
& not the part without the leave of said Court on being otherwise legally discharged.

          Joshua M. Coffee
                    vs   Motion - Came the plaintiff by attorney and on motion
          Augustine Robinson   of the plaintiff by his atto. and it appearing to the
satisfaction of the Court that a Judgment has been obtained by the Chairman and
board of Carmon School Commissioners against the said Augustine as principal and
James Goodner and the said Joshua M. Coffee as his securities for the sum of fifty
seven dollars and fifty six cents and it appearing then to the Court by the Sheriff's
Receipt filed, that said Joshua M. Coffee has paid the sum of twenty eight dollars
and seventy eight cents part of the Judgment aforesaid - whereupon on motion It is
considered by the Court that the said Joshua M. Coffee recover against the said
Augustine Robinson the sum of twenty eight dollars seventy eight cents ($28.78)
the amt so paid by him as aforesaid for said Robinson, and also the costs of this
motion.

P 184   James Shelton administrator of Arch. Frith decd. vs James Read   Case
          Came the plaintiff by his attorney and the defendant in proper person and the
defendant here in open Court confesses Judgment in favour of the plaintiff for the
sum of sixty nine dollars and ninety cents. It is therefore considered by the Court
that the plaintiff recover against the defendant the aforesaid sum of sixty nine
dollars and ninety cents and the costs of suit.

          Jonathan Picketts
                    vs   Debt - Came the defendant by their attornies and suggests
          Wright and Newby   the death of the plaintiff.

          The State of Tennessee
                    vs   Indictment A. & B. - Came the attorney General who
          Wilson Boulton   prosecutes for the state and the defendant in proper
person and on motion of the defendant by his counsel a Rule is admitted him to show
cause who this Indictment in this case should be quashed, and said motion to quash
being argued by the counsel on both sides and mature deliberation had thereon by
the Court. It is considered by the Court that the costs in this cause be taxed to
The attorney General Samuel Yerger.

          The State of Tennessee
                    vs   Presentment Gaming - Came the Attorny General for
          Braxton M. Key   the state and the defendant in proper person and the
defendant pleads Guilty to the presentment & for his trial puts himself upon the
mercy of the Court. It is It is therefore considereddby the Court that the defendant pay a fine of five dollars ($5) and the costs of this prosecution fine and
costs paid $21.90.

P 185   Court adjourns until tomorrow morning 9 oclock.

                                                  Enum Whitley
                                                  S. D. McMurry
                                                  Henry B. Mahana Jr

Saturday morning Court meet pursuant to adjournment. Present Esqr. McDonald, Whitley and McMurry.

Ordered that Lat Hagard pay a single Tax on 226 acres of deeded land, 5 town lots and 6 negroes paid.

On motion ordered by the Court that the Clerk of this County and the Sheff. of Smith County.

P 186   Saturday morning 28th November 1835 Court met pursuant to adjournment present Saml. D. McMurry,
     Exum Whitley and
     Henry B. McDonald.

Josiah Whitley tenders to the Court his resignation of the office of Constable which is by the Court accepted.

On motion ordered that Lat Hagard pay a single Tax on 226 acres of land, Town lots, and 6 negroes paid.

The Grand Jury came into Court and made presentment against John McGee overseer of Road, also a presentment against Thomas Durham overseer of Road ordered that capias issue.

State
vs   Presentment overseer Road came the attorney General for
Mathew Nichols   the state and the Defendant in proper person the defendant being arraigned upon the presentment Pleads not guilty thereto and for his trial puts himself upon the country and the attorney General doth the like. Then came a Jury of good and lawful men to wit Horace Oliver, Caleb Read, Champman T. Thomas, Edward Evans, Lemuel Turney, Jonathan Fuston, Gregory Moore, Wm. Reeves, Winston Chandler, Stirling Jackson, Moses Reeves & Andrew W. Jouvanseau, who being elected tried and sworn the truth to speak upon the issue joined upon their oath do say that the defendant is guilty in manner and form as charged in the presentments It is therefore considered by the Court that the defendant pay a fine of five dollars and the cost of this prosecution and that the defendant be and remain in the custody of the Sheriff until the fine and costs are secured or paid.

John B. Forester who had been appointed one of the executors in the last will and Testament of Stephen Roberson decd. renounced his right to execute said will which renunciation was made in writing and ordered by the Court to be filed as of record.

P 187   The Grand Jury came into Court and made a presentment against Michael Ethridge, Milly Taylor, Lydia Hail, for open and notorious Lewdness and returned to consider of further business and capias are ordered to issue against siad defendant

George Sutton
vs   Deed of conveyance for 70 acres of land lying in Smith
Daniel Goad   County on the waters of Paytons Creek bearing date the 18 of November 1835 was produced in open Court and was duly acknowleged by George Sutton the Bargainor and on motion ordered to be certified for Registration.

On motion ordered that Elijah Haynie George W. Royster and Benjamin Piper, be appointed commissioner to settle with Andrew Payne, administrator of Bolin Vaughn decd. and make report to next Court.

State
vs   This cause is continued on affidavit of the Defendant
Wm Calhoon   until Tuesday next.

State   Contuned. until Tuesday next by consent. Josiah Whitley
  vs   cost̄h proved 6 days attendance Mathew Nichol a Juror proved
B. C. Dixon
3 days attendance & 2 Ferriages.

                                     Samuel D. McMurry
                                     Exum Whitley
                                     Henry B. McDonald.

P 188   Monday morning Court meet pursuant to agreement present Esqrs.McDonald,
                                                     Whitley,
                                                    McMurry,
                                                      Brevard,
                                                    Sutton,
                                                      Herod,
                                                    Thompson,
                                                      Cornwell,
                                                    Goodall,
                                                      Dixon.

     On motion ordered that Joseph Bradford be appointed Overseer of the Road in-
stead of Samuel Walker and have the same hands and bonds(bounds).

     Ordered that William Kelly be appointed Overseer of the Road instead of John
H. Burford and have the same hands and bounds.

     John Lancaster and Jad Cheatham Esqrs. appointed to apportion the hands to
H. L. Stephens Overseer of the road report that the following persons and hands work
under said Overseer towit - William Jones, Charles Stevens, Henry Stevens, Federick
Stevens, John Exum, Jno. McGinnis, Lawson Slinkard, Solomon Wiatt, Stephen Hickmans,
Joseph Petty, John Lamberson, Robert Lamberson, Nicholas Braswell Edward Bennett,
Sterling Hilton, Thomas Lamberson and hand which said report is by the court confirmed

     The following list of hands were appointed to work under Thomas A. Flippin
overseer of the Road from the Bridge at Rome to Robert Kinnys to wit. Joseph Bridges,
William Reeves, Tilman Flippin, John Hazard, G. Flippin, R. C. Vetal, Martin(Mastin?)
Freeman, I. T. Owens, Noles Purnell, William Douglass, Francis Price, M. Rise, John
P 189 F R. Hazard, John Hazard, M. G. Owens, H. G. Owens, James Green, O. Purnell,
John S. Rowels, James Pope, I. B. Hodges, S. O. Pope, Dempsey Sute, M. Dyson & hands,
John Williams, James Mates, John Mates, E. Clark, John Sute, S. Heirs, James Crage,
James Newby, John Gann, Enoch Gann, Henry Highers, T. R. C. Norris, A. Jouvanceau,
D. C. Ward and hand W. Rigsby, A. Sinder Wilson Buts Mrs. M. Friths hands - It is
ordered by the Court that said hand work under said Overseer.

     Ordered that Josiah Marshall be appointed Overseer of the Road in the stead
of John Raullins(?) and have the same hands and bounds.

     Ordered that William McGinnis be appointed Overseer of the Road in the
stead of Willis Coggin and have the same hands and bounds.

     Elihu H. Greer
         To   Deed of conveyance 84 acres 3 rods and 20 poles bearing
  Thomas M. P. Hall   date 25 May 1835 from Elihu H. Greer to Thomas M. P. Hall
lying in Smith County, was produced in open Court and was duly proven by the oath of
Wesley Oglesby and Stephen A. Oglesby subscribing witness to the same and on motion
ordered to be certified for Registration.

P 190   Daniel Smith
         To   Deed of conveyance for 50 acres of land from Daniel
  Daniel Huddleston   Smith to Daniel Huddleston bearing date the 23 day
of November 1835 was produced in open Court and was duly acknowledged by Daniel
Smith the Bargainor and on motion ordered to be certified for Registration.

George C. Gifford
To
Moses Freeman

Deed of conveyance for 90 acres of land lying in Smith County from George C. Gifford to Moses Freeman was produced in open Court, and was duly proven by the oaths of Hiram H. Johnson and A. G. ford subscribing witnesses thereto and on motion ordered to be certified for Rigistration.

P 191   George C. Gifford
to
Moses Freeman

Deed of conveyance for 10 acres of land lying in Smith County on the East Fork of Goose Creek bearing date the 7 day of July 1835 was produced in open Court and was duly proven by the oaths of Hiram H. Johnson subscribing witness thereto and on motion ordered to be certified for Registration.

The administrator of John Johnson ded. render into Court an act of sales of said dec. Estate which on motion is ordered to be recorded.

The administrators of Joseph Fuller ded. rendered into Court an Inventory on act. of sales, and on motion ordered to be recorded.

The Commissioners appointed to lay off and set apart a years provision to the widow & family of Joseph Fuller ded. made their report which is ordered to be recorded.

The administrator of Samuel Piper decd. rendered into Court an Inventory and act. of sales of said ded. Estate which on motion is ordered to be recorded.

On motion M. L. West, Willie Jones, Jonathan Griffith be appointed Commissioners to lay off and set apart a years provision to the widown and family of John M. Bennett ded. and make report to next Court.

P 192   On motion the Executor of James C. Coleman ded. rendered into Court and Inventory of the said decased. Estate, which on motion is ordered to be recorded.

The administrator of Archibald G. Braswell ded. rendered into Court an Inventory an act. of Sales of said ded. Estate which on motion is ordered to recorded.

Mahala Pharis is appointed administratrix of the estate of Rubin Faris decd. who came into Court and qualified and together with Winston Beck entered into bond in the sum of two hundred dollars conditioned as the law directs - Letters of administration is granted on said ded. Estate.

The administratrix of the estate of Rubin Faris decd. rendered into Court an inventory of the estate of said decd. which is ordered to be recorded.

Edward Evans is appointed overseer of the road in the place Benjamin Blades and have the same hands and Bounds.

Josiah Moses Henry Beasley and Jeremiah Belk are appointed Commissioners to settle with James Pendarvis's executor of the last will and testament of Henry Dickins decd. and Administrator of the estate Thomas vanse decd.

On motion William Petty William Woods James Lee be appointed Commissioners to settle with Samuel Fitzpatrick administrator of Rebecca Ballard ded. and make report to next Court.

P 193   Daniel Smith is appointed administrator of the estate of Jesse West ded. who came into Court and qualified together with his securities Benjamin Piper and Samuel Oldham and entered into bond in the sum of four hundred dollars conditioned as the law directs. Letters of administration is granted on said ded. Estate.

William Patterson is appointed administrator of the estate of John M. Bennett ded. who came into Court and qualified together with his securites William Bennett Jr. and William Bennett Sr. and entered into Bond in the sum of fifteen hundred dollars conditioned as the law directs. Letters of administration is granted on said ded. Estate.

John Moore is appointed administrator of the Estate of Thomas Moore ded. who came into Court and qualified together with his securities, John Moore, Jesse Fuller, and Gregory Moore and entered into Bond in the sum of six thousand dollars conditioned as the law directs. Letters of administration granted on said ded. Estate.

The Executor of the last will and Testament of David Douglass ded. rendered into Court an inventory and act of sales of the said ded. estate which is ordered to be recorded.

The administration of the estate of John Baker decd. returned into Court a supplementary inventory of the estate of said decd. which is ordered to be recorded.

Brice F. Martin Saml. D. McMurray & Thomas Phelps are appointed Commissioners to set apart and lay off one years provision for the widow and family of William Walker ded, and make report to next Court.

P 194   Alfred A. Brevard and Archibald Thompson who were appointed Commissioners to superintend the building of a Bridge across the mouth of Taylors Branch on Goose Creek made their report which is confined by the Court and ordered to be recorded. And it is further ordered by the Court that an order and certified issue to Hiram Haunshell for the sum of one hundred and fifteen dollars to be paid by the County trustee out of any money in his hands not otherwise appropriated, the same having been heretofore appropriated.

The commissioners appointed to lay off & set apart and year's provisions for the widow and family of Henry H. Taylor decd. made this report and the same is ordered to be recorded.

Robert Hodges, John Turner, and Wesley Mates are appointed Commissioners to settle with James Shelton, administrator of the estate of Archibald Frith decd. relative to the Guardianship of John I. Varser a Deaf & Dumb man of whom the said Archd. Frith was guardian at the time of his death, and that they make report to next bounds.

The administrator of Levi Oliver rendered into Court an inventory and account of sales of the estate of said decd which is ordered to be recorded.

The last will testament of Charles Nixon decd. was produced in open Court and the due execution thereof was proven by the oaths of Hazard P. Cleveland and William Gregory the subscribing witness thereto which is ordered to be recorded. and thereupon came Leonard Ballow and Mary Nixon, who were two of the persons appointed executrix & executor in said last will and Testament and renounced their right to execute said Last will and Testament and William Nixon and John Nixon the other persons appointed executors in said last will & testament came into Court and qualified and together with Benjamin Piper, James Piper, and Samuel Oldham their securities entered into bond in the sum of ten thousand dollars conditioned as the law directs and Letters Testamentary is granted then on sd. estate.

P 195   The Commissioners appointed to lay off and set apart a years provision for the widow and family of John Johnson decd. made their report which is ordered to be recorded.

The Commissioners appointed to settle with the executor of the last will and testament of Solomon Key decd. made their report which is confined by the Court and ordered to be recorded and it is further ordered by the Court that the said Executor be allowed the sum of thirty five dollars as a reasonable compensation for his trouble and services in administering said estate to be retained by him of the said estate in his hands.

The Jurors summoned by the Sheriff to lay off to the widow of John Johnson decd. her dower out of the real estate of said John Johnson decd made their report which is ordered to recorded and It is considered by the Court that Grace Johnson the petitioner pay the costs acrued on said petition and process.

Ordered that John Lucas William I. Bennett Thomas A. Lancaster be appointed Commissioners to settle with Ira B. Cowan adms. de bonis non of the Estate of Joshua Conger ded. and report to this Court.

The Commissioners appointed to lay off and set apart a years provision to the widow and family of Sim Oliver, ded. made this report which is ordered to be recorded.

On motion ordered that Andrew Payne be released from all further liability as Guardian for Rubin Hass, after he settle his Guardianship and return also The effects now in his hands belonging to the said Hall to him.

P 196   The administrator of John Craig ded. rendered into Court an Inventory and act of Sale of said ded. Estate which on motion is ordered to be recorded.

Ordered that Exum Whitly David Tyrad, Alexander James be appointed commissioners to settle with William Hall, adms. of John Briant ded. and make report to next Court.

The Executor of Francis Cornwell ded. render into Court a supplementary inventory which is ordered to be recorded.

On motion John H. Burford James T. Murford and Crud(?) Penn be appointed Commissioners to settle with Solomon dice adms. of Henry Dice ded. and make report to next Court.

Proclamation having been made the Court proceeded to the election of Constables and to that office did elect D.M. Johnson in Captain Harper Company Charles I. Bratton in Captain Brattons Company John Paty in Captain Whitley Company who came into Court and qualified, and severally entered into bond together with their P 197   securities in the sum 1000 dollars each conditioned as the law directs.

The Last will and testament of Jesse Coleman was produced in open Court and duly proven by the oaths of William P. Hughes and William McDonald subscribing witnesses thereto and on motion ordered to be recorded.

The administrator of the estate of Daniel Batton decd. made his report to Court of the sale of a tract of land belonging to said decd's estate, under an order of last court which report is ordered to be recorded.

Elisha Walker is appointed administrator of the estate of William Walker decd. who came into Court and together with John A. Johnson & John McMurray his securities entered into bond in the sum of two thousand dollars conditioned as the law directs. and letters of administration is granted him on said estate.

Daniel Smith
　　To
　Silas C. Cornwell ｝ Deed for 4 Acres of land lying in the county of Smith on Defeated Creek from Daniel Smith to Silas C. Cornwell was produced in open Court and the execution thereof was duly acknowledged by the Daniel Smith the bargainor and on motion the same is ordered to be certified for Registration.

It is ordered that the following persons good and lawful men of Smith County be summoned the Sheriff of said county to attend as Juror at the April Term of the Circuit for said County 1836 to wit Elijah Carmon, Joseph Cartwright, Simon P. Hughes, John Stuart, John McFarland, Thomas Phelps, Brice F. Martin, Joel Cheatham, Thomas Harper, Rubin Evans, Josha Bratton, James Yeargin, William Bennet Wm. Floyd, Willis McEachern, Wesley Harvey, Godfrey Gregory, Thomas Gregory, Sampson Sloan, Exum Whitley Mathew Harper Patrick Firgusson, John Wilson Thomas B. Day and William Kyle and Benjamin Avent Constables to attend said Circuit Court, and that a Venire facias issue &C.

Ordered that the Sheriff summon the following persons good and lawful men of Smith County to attend as Jurors at the next term of this Court to wit Richard Alexander, Richard Chambers Daniel M. Ellison, James Gwaltney Timothy Walton Senr. Robert Pursley Gideon Gifford, John Duncan William Hall, Thomas Walker, Solomon P 198 Dice, Reubin Turner, Samuel Winkler, Thomas Gregory, Alexander McKinnis, William Strother, Daniel Wilkerson, Benjamin Wootton, Dickie Ward, Jeriks(?) Kemp, James C. Williams, Martin R. Bains, James W. Bransford, Buckner S. Cardwell, and William Dawson and Robert Nixon Constables to wait upon said Court, and that a Venire facias issue &C.

Ordered the following persons be appointed to take the list of taxable property and polls in the following Captains Companies for the year 1836 to wit:

John B. Hughes	Esqr.	in	Capt.	Murry (?)	Company
Thomas W. Casley	"	"	"	McFarlands	do
Joel Cheatham	"	"	"	Harpin's	do
M. L. West	"	"	"	Harrison's	do
Thomas Patterson	"	"	"	Smith's	do
H. B. McDonald	"	"	"	Tregg's	do
Nep. Durham	"	"	"	Cowan's	do
A. A. Brevard	"	"	"	Duncan's	do
Isaac Beaty	"	"	"	Warford's	do
John Tubb	"	"	"	Payne's	do
Exum Whitley	"	"	"	Whitley's	do
James Goodner	"	"	"	T. I. Tyrees	do
A. Overall	"	"	"	Jenkins	do
John Micaw(?)	"	"	"	Donoho's	do
John Henderson	"	"	"	May's	do
D. A. McEachern	"	"	"	Moore's	do
Silas Pinkley	"	"	"	Turvins	do
Benjamin Turner	"	"	"	White's	do
Archd. Thompson	"	"	"	Meador's	do
George Sutton	"	"	"	Wilkerson's	do
Peter Herod	"	"	"	Parker's	do
Reubin Evans	"	"	"	Fuston's	do
Exum Whitley	"	"	"	Harvis	do
Isaac Goodall	"	"	"	Oliver's	do
David Hogg	"	"	"	Reece	do
Silas C. Cornwell	"	"	"	William's	do
Isaac Goodall	"	"	"	Hudson's	do
Saml. D. McMurry	"	"	"	Johnson's	do
Zachry Ford	"	"	"	Scruggs	do
Patrick Firguson	"	"	"	Saunders	do
John Lancaster	"	"	"	T. T. Tyree'sdo	

P 199   John I. Bennett is permitted to pay a single Tax on 1 white pole and 2 Town Lots. O. B. Hubbard 1 B. P, pd. Turner Wilkerson 55 acres land pd.

Henry B. McDonald is appointed agent of the Chairman and board of Cannon School Commissioners who came into Court and entered into bond together with O. B. Hubbard, Samuel P. Harvand John G. Park, Archibald W. Overton and Abraham H. King his securities in the sum of thirty two thousand five hundred dollars conditioned as the law directs.

Sarah Scott   §   Petition For Dower
vs   §
The Heirs of Moses Scott decd. §

    Came the petitioner by her atts and upon hearing of the matter of the
petition and it appearing to the court that all the heirs of intestate, and the
administrators have acknowledged service of petition, waived all motion and
consented for the court to proceed upon the petition at this term. It is thereupon ordered by the court, that the Sheriff of this County summon a jury of five
free holders unconnected with any of the parties interested either by affinity
consanquanity who upon oath shall allot and set of to the petitioner her
dower in and of the land in the petition mentioned, pursuant to the directions
of the statutes in such case made & provided &c and that a writ issue &c.

Mary Jourvanceau   §
vs.   §   Petition for Dower
The Heirs of John Jourvanceau Decd. §

    Came the petitioner by her atts when it appeared to the court, that Nancy
Rebecca, Elizabeth, Mary, Benjamin, Barry, S. & Matilda C. Jourvanceau children
of said deceased are minors & have no general guardian and that Mary Jourvanceau
Junr. a grand daughter of intestate a daughter of a deceased son John Jourvanceau
Junr. is also a minor and has no general guardian, on motion Andrew W. Jourvanceau
is appointed guardian ad litem for all of said minor distributors & heirs of
intestate to defend this petition and the said Andrew W. guardian as aforesaid
and administrator &c of said John J Jourvanceau decesd. having acknowledged
service of petition all notice, and consented for dower to be assigned or prayed
for It is thereupon ordered by the court that the Sheriff of this county summons
a jury of five freeholders unconnected with any of the parties interested either
by affinity or consanquanity who upon oath shall allot and set off to the
petition her dower in and of the land in the petition mentioned pursuant to the
directions of the statistics in such case made and provided &c and that a writ
issue &c.

P 200   The Executor of the last will and testament of Patrick Donoho decd
rendered into court on inventory of said decd's estate which is ordered to be
becorded.

Court adjourned until tomorrow morning 10 O'clock
                                  Samuel D McMurray
                                  Henry B McDonald
                                  Exum Whitley

    Tuesday morning 1st decr. 1835. Court met pursuant to adjournment present
Exum Whitly Henry B. McDonald and Samuel D. McMurray Esqrs Justices.

Simon P. Hughes Richard Alexander and James Shelton are appointed commissioners
to settle with Robert Hodges and John B. Armstrong administrator with the will
annexed of Berryman Turner senr. decd. that said settlement shall be made at
such time between this and the next term of this court as said commissioners or anyone of them shall appoint said settlement to be made at the House of Hubbard &
Seay or same other house in Rome and notice from anyone or more of said commissioners of the time & place of said settlement shall be sufficient and binding upon
either of the parties administrators aforesaid; and said commissioners are
directed to make report of said settlement to the next term of this court.

    The administrators of the estate of Berryman Turner senr. decd. rendered
into court on inventory and accounty of sales of the estate of said decd. whcih
on motion is ordered to be recorded.

P 201   On motion John McCall is appointed Guardian to Robert McCall who thereupon came into court and together with David McCall and O B Hubbard entered into bond in the sum of three thousand dollars conditioned as the law directs.

On motion John G. Brien is appointed Guardian of Joseph Y. Stuart who came into court and together with P. W. Brien and Saml. P. Howard entered into bond in the sum of three hundred dollars conditioned as the law directs.

The commissioners appointed to lay off and set apart one years provision for the widow and family Geraldus Linch decd made their report which is ordered to be recorded.

John B. Armstrong &   Deed for 96 acres of land from John B. Armstrong Nancy
Nancy Armstrong &   Robert Hodges Armstrong and John Turner to Robert
John Turner   Hodges bearing date 1st day of December 1835 was this
To   day produced in open court and the execution thereof
Robert Hodges   was duly acknowledged in open court by John B. Armstrong
and John Turner two of the Bargainers and on motion a commissione is awarded and ordered to issue directed to William W. Seay and Thomas I. Hubbard to take the prvy examination of Nancy Armstrong the other bargainors and that they report their examination of said Nancy Armstrong to the next term of this court.

Robert Hodges
Elizabeth Hodges &   Deed for 125 acres lying in Smith County on Round Lick
John Turner   creek Bearing date 1st day of December 1835. Nancy
To   Armstrong from Robert Hodges, Elizabeth Hodges and John
John B. Armstrong   Turner to John B. Armstrong and Nancy Armstrong was this
day produced in open court and the execution thereof was duly acknowledged in open court and the execution thereof was duly acknowledged in open court by John Turner and Robert Hodges, two of the bargainors; and on motion a commission is awarded directed to Thomas J. Hubbard and William W Seay to take the privy examination of Elizabeth Hodge, the other bargainor, touching her voluntary execution of said deed of conveyance and that they report their examination to next court.

P 202   John B. Armstrong
         Nancy Armstrong   Deed for 40 acres of land lying in Smith County
         Robert Hodges   on Round Lick creek bearing 1st Decr. 1835 from
         Elizabeth Hodges   John B. Armstrong, Nancy Armstrong, Robert Hodges,
         To   and Elizabeth Hodges to John Turner was produced
         John Turner   in open court and the execution thereof was duly
acknowledged in open was duly acknoweleged in open court by John B. Armstrong and Hodges two of the bargainors to said deed, and on motion a commission is awarded. directed to Thomas I. Hubbard and William W. Seay to take the privy examination of Nancy Armstrong and and Elizabeth Hodges the other two Bargainors to said deed touching their voluntary execution of said deed of conveyance and that they the said commissioners report to next court &c

John B. Armstrong
To   Deed for 52 acres of land lying in Smith County bearing
Moses Easter   date 29th November 1835 from John B. Armstrong to Moses
Estos was this day produced in open court and the execution thereof was duly acknowleged by John B. Armstrong the bargainor and on motion the same is ordered to be certified for Registration

Tilman Norris
To
Moses Eastes

Deed for Town Lot in Rome Smith County Known in the place of said town by No 18
deed bearing date the 9th day of January 1835 from Tilman Norris to Moses Estes
was this day produced in open court and the execution thereof was duly proven
by the oaths of William B. Moore and John W. Eastes subscribing witnesses
thereto and on motion the same is ordered to certified for Registration

Samuel Birdine }
To   } Deed of conveyance for one town lot No. 17 in the town of
Moses Estes } Rome Smith County from Samuel Birdine to Moses Estes bearing
p204 date the 14th day of April 1834 was produced in open court and the execution
thereof was duly proved in open court by the oaths of William B. Moore and John
W. Estes the subscribing witness thereto and on motion the same is ordered to be
certified for Registration.

James Shelton administrator of the estate of Archibald Frith decd }
vs }
Solomon McGee
    Case come the parties by their attorney and thereupon came a jury of good
and lawful men towit: Horace Oliver, Cable Read Edward Evans Jeremiah Gammon, Jonathan Fuston, Winston Candler, Gregory Moore, William Reeves, Andrew W. Jovanceau,
Sterling Jackson, Moses Reeves, John T. Stokes who being elected tried and sworn
well and truly to try the matter of the appeal in this cause between the parties
upon their oath do say that they find the issue in favour of the plaintiff and
they further say they affirm the Judgement of the Justice of the peace in this
cause. It is therefore considered by the court that the plaintiff recover against
the defendant the sum of twelve dollars sixty and one half cents the amount of the
Judgment of the Justice of the Peace also the further sum of one dollar and
fifty seven and one half cents being the interest after the rate of 12½ per cent
per annum which has accrued thereon since the date of the Peace, making in all
the sum of fourteen dollars and eighteen cents $14.18, also the cost of suit

Jacob S. Johnson John P. Johnson Wilson T. Meadow and Susannah his wife Warrin
P. Coker and Mary his wife and Jacob S. Johnson Guardian ad Litem for Thomas D.
Andrew J. William C. & Willis P. Johnson Minors and All being the heirs at Law
of John Johnson deceased.   Exparte
    Pit for Division of land came the petitioners by their atto and presented their
petition in open court which being read is ordered to be filed and on motion it
is further ordered by the court that Alfred A. Brevard John Rankin, Joseph F.
Hibbit, Cyrus W. Brevard, and William C. Bransford are appointed commissioners
and Alexander Fergusson is appointed surveyor to accompany said commissioners
to decide and make petition between said heirs and distributers of the lands and
real estate of John Johnson deceased and often the said commissioners shall have
been duly sworn by some Justice of the peace for said County they will proceed
P204 by actual survey to make partition and division as aforesaid of the lands
aforesaid between the parties aforesaid setting forth with as much procession as
practicable the specific boundaries description of each distribution share on
position having a due regard to quality and quantity taking care to charge the
more valuable dividend or dividends with such seem or sums of money as they
in their best discretion shall adjudge to be just and properto be paid to the
dividend or dividends of more inferior value and when said commissioners shall
have made said division and set apart and alloted to each distributee his or
her tract or lot with as much accuracy and Justice as practicable they will certify
their proceedings herein under their hands and seals to the next term of this
court.

The Grand Jury came into court and made a presentment against Thomas Bradford
overseer of the road ordered that a capias issue against said defendant.

Jacob S. Johnson is appointed Guardian ad litem of Thomas D. Andrew J. William C
and Willis P. Johnson minor children of John Johnson deceased to superintend the

interest of said minors in relation to the pet'tion this day filed for the devision
and partition of the real estate of said decd.

The State |
     vs | Affray - Came the atto. Genl. for the state and the defen-
Peck W. Brien | dant in proper person and the deft. being arraigned on the
presentment pleads guilty thereto and for his trial puts himself on the mercy of
the Court. It is therefore considered by the Court that the deft. pay a fine of
two dollars and fifty cents and the costs of this prosecution, and Robert Allen
here in open Court acknowledges himself indebted for the fine and costs aforesaid
and that execution was against him jointly with the deft. for the fine and costs
aforesaid.

State vs Mathew McMartin ordered that aplunums(?) capias issue.

P 205   State |
     vs | Presentment Gaming - Came the atto. General for the State
     Bird Read | and the defendant by his counsel and this cause is con-
tinued in the affidavit of the atto. Genl. until next term. And then Caleb Read
herein open Court and acknowledges himself indebted to the State of Tennessee in
the sum of two hundred and fifty dollars to levied of his goods and chattels lands
and tenements to be void on condition that the defendant Bird Read make his personal appearance and before the next Court of Pleas and quarter sessions to be
held for the county of Smith at the Court house in Carthage on the first Wednesday
after the fourth Monday in February next to answer the said State are the above
charge of unlawful gaming and not depart without leave of said Courts.

State |
     vs | Presentment - Overseer of the Road came the atto. Genl. for
Levi Squires | the state and the deft. in proper person, and the defendant
pleads guilty to the presentment, and puts himself on the mercy of the Court. It
is therefore considered by the Court that the deft. pay a fine of two dollars and
fifty cents and the costs of this prosecution.

Andrew W. Jouvanceau Champ. T. Thomas Jurors and Josiah Davidson Grand Juror
are discharged from further attendance as Jurors at this term and each of them
prove 6 days attendance on 4 ferriages.

James Shelton admr. &C |
     vs | Case - Came the parties by their attornies and
. Eneah Gann | thereupon came a Jury of good and lawful men to
wit Horace Oliver, Caleb Read, Edward Evans, Jeremiah Gammon, Jonathan Fuston, Gregory Moore, William Reeves, Winston Candler, Sterling Jackson, Moses Reeves, John
T. Stokes & Isaac Linch who being elected tried and sworn the truth to speak upon
the issue Joined. and after hearing a part of the testimony in this cause and
because this cause cannot be finished this day the Jurors aforesaid are permitted
to dispense and meet again tomorrow morning at 9 oclock.

P 206   Hiram H. Johnson |
     vs | Attachment   - Came the plaintiff by his attorney
    Robert D. Hoover | and the defendant being solemnly called came not
but made default. It is therefore considered by the court that the plaintiff recover against the defendant one hundred and fifty three dollars twenty eight cents
the debt in the plaintiff declaration mentioned also the costs of suit and it is
further considered by the court that the property build upon under the attachment
in this cause be sold by the sheriff to satisfy the plaintiff's debt and costs
aforesaid.

The Grand Jury made presentments against Orville Green and Thomas B. Dillon
overseers of the road. Ordered that capias issue against said deft.

The administrator of the estate of Judith Nunby decd. rendered into Court an inventory and account of sales of said estate, which is ordered to be recorded.

State
vs
William Calhoun

Presentment Gamin - Came the atto. General for the state and the defendant in proper person and this cause is continued on the affidavit of the attorney General. And the said defendant and David A. Crenshaw here in open Court acknowledges themselves to owe and stand indebted to the state of Tennessee in the sum of two hundred and fifty dollars each to be levied of their respective goods goods and chattels lands and tenements for the use of the state to be void on condition that the said William Calhoun shall make his personal appearance. before this court at the next term to be held for the County of Smith at the Court house in Carthage on the first Wednesday after the fourth Monday in February next to answer the state on the above charge of unlawful gaming and not depart without being legally discharged.

P 207   State
vs
James Jones

Presentment Gaming - Came the attorney General for the State and the defendant in proper person and this cause is continued on the affidavit of the atto. Genl. And then came the defendant and Caleb Read here in open Court and acknowledged themselves indebted to the state of Tennessee in the sum of two hundred and fifty dollars each to be levied of their respective goods and chattels lands and tenements for the use of said state to be void on condition that the defendant make his personal appearance before this Court house in Carthage on the first Wednesday after the fourth Monday in February next to answer the state on the above charge for unlawful Gaming and not depart without the leave of said Court.

State
vs
Don C. Dixon

Presentment Gaming - Came the attorney Genl. for the state and the defendant in proper person and this cause in continued on the affidavid of the Atto. Genl. And then came the defendant and Archibald W. Overton(?) here in open Court acknowledged themselves indebted to the state in the sum of two hundred and fifty dollars each to levied of their respective goods and chattels land and tenements for the use of the state to be void on condition that the said defendant make his personal appearance before this Court at the next term to be held for the County of Smith at the Courthouse in Carthage on the first Wednesday after the fourth Monday in February next to answer the state on the above charge of unlawful gaming and not depart without the leave of said Court.

P 208   Court adjourns until tomorrow morning 9 oclock.

Henry B. McDonald
Samuel D. McMurry
Exum Whitley.

Wednesday morning 2nd Decr. 1835. Court met pursuant adjournment present Henry B. McDonald, Exum Whitley & Samuel D. McMurry Esquires.

John Baker admr. &C.
vs
Enoch Gann

Debt - Came the parties by their attorneys and Simon P. Hughes Harvey Hogg and John G. Park arbitrators to whom the matters in controversy in this suit was refined at the last term of this Court came here into open Court and filed their award which is in the words and figures following to wit - "Smith County, State of Tennessee, we the undersigned appointed as arbitrators by an ordere of the County Court of Smith to arbitrate the matters in difference submitted to us in the case of John Baker admr. &C. of John Baker, decd. against Enoch Gann, and after examining all the testimony pro-

P 209   duced before before us by the parties and after deliberation on the same could not agree and called in an umpire John G. Park who examined the testimony examined by us after which we with the aid of said umpire award as follows viz- that the vote given by defendant Enoch Gann - was given without consideration and for that is well and void; and that said Gann be discharged from the payment thereof".   "Signed"   S. P. Hughes
                                                   Harvey Hogg   Arbitrators
                                                   John G. Park, Umpire.

Which said award is now here made the Judgment of this Court It is therefore further considered by the Court that said plaintiff take nothing by his suit. that the defendant be discharged and go hence without day. And John Gann here in open Court assumes the payment of all the costs of this suit.

James Bealy, Spencer Kelly, and Peter Reynolds are appointed commissioners to settle with James Tubb admr. of the estate of Guy Lee decd. and make report to next Courts.

The commissioners appointed to settle with Ira B. Cowan admr. de bonis non of Joshua Conger decd. made their report which is ordered to be recorded.

Spencer Kelly is appointed administrator with the will annuled of Stephen Robinson decd. who came into Court and qualified and together with William B. Stokes John T. Stoker, James Tubb and John Conger his securities and entered into bond in the sum of twenty five thousand dollars conditioned as the law directs. and letters of administration is granted him said estate.

James Shelton admr. &C. |
         vs | Case - Came the parties by their attornies and
John Gann | this cause is continued until next term, and on
motion a commission is awarded him to take the deposition of James K. Foster of Franklin County Illinois are giving the plaintiff 30 days notice of the time and 10 days notice if taken in this county.

P 210   Lemuel Turney a Juror at the present term is excused from further attendance as a Juror & proved 7 days & 4 ferriage.

The Grand Jury came into Court and made presentments against Hezakiah Stevens, Alfred Betty, John Robinson, overseers of Roads. the Grand Jury also made presentments against John Minton, James Barret & Alexander James for unlawful Gaming ordered that a capias issue against each of said defendants.

William Mathews |
      To | Deed for 100 acres of land lying in Smith County bearing
William Petty | date 24th day of October 1831. From William Mathews
William Petty was this day produced in open Court and the execution thereof was duly proven in open Court by the oaths of James P. McKee and David Haynes the subscribing witnesses thereto and on motion the same is ordered to be certified for Registered.

Ordered that O. B. Hubbard John G. Park and Andrew Allison be appointed Commissioners or any two of them to make settlement with and receive from John I. Burnett clerk of this court or from Andrew Pickett and Samuel P. Howard administrators of Jonathan Pickett decd. all the books bonds, note, vouchers, Receipts or evidence of money- that maybe in or belonging to the Agency of the Common Shool(school?) fund for Smith County. and that they make an inventory of all the money notes and bonds in said Agency, and that they record the same in the record book of said Agency. stating the number of the notes the amount of each and the names of the principal and security to each note, and security to each note, and if any is deemed bad or doubtful, that they make such reference, in order that it may be know, what is the state and condition of the funds at the time of said settlement and that said commissioners attest the same with their own proper signatures for future inspection and so soon as said commissioners shall have made out the inventory and performed the other duties above specified they will deliver over all the books papers, bonds, notes, vouchers & money belonging to said agency, to Henry B. McDonald, agent appointed at the present term of this P 211 Court, and take his receipt for the same. This order is drawn up by the agent and requested of the Court to have the same spread upon the minuts of this Court, as the agent wishes the people of this County to know the true situation of their school funds when the same shall come to his hands - and the agent wishes this order to be recorded in the books of the agency by the commissioners together with the inventory and other proceedings aforesaid.

James Shelton admr.
      vs   Case — Came again the parties by their attorneys and
Enoch Gann   also the same Jury who were elected, tried and sworn in this cause on yesterday and after hearing further testimony in this cause and because the same cannot be finished on this day the Juror aforesaid are permitted to dispense until tomorrow morning 9 oclock.   Saml. D. McMurry
                                            Henry B. McDonald
                                            Exum Whitley

Thursday morning 3rd Decr. 1835 - Court met pursuant adjournment present Exum Whitley,
Henry B. McDonald and
Samuel D. McMurry Esquires.

James Shelton admr of the estate of A. Frith decd
                                     Case - came again the
                 vs   parties by their atto's.
Enoch Gann
and also the same Jury elected impannelled and sworn in this cause on the day before yesterday - upon their oaths do say they find the issues in favour of the plaintiff and they do assess the plaintiff's damages occasioned by the non performance of the assumptions and promises in the declaration mentioned to forty six dollars thirty seven cents. It is therefore considered by the Court that the plaintiff recover against the defendant the aforesaid sum of forty six dollars and thirty seven cents ($46.37) the damages by the Jury aforesaid, in manner and form aforesaid assessed and his costs by him about his suit in this behalf expended.

P 212   Manson M. Brien, James Tubb & John S. Brion
                     vs   Debts - Came the plaintiffs
        Martin Shoemake and Benjamin E. West   by their attorneys and the defendants being solemnly called came not but made default. It is therefore considered by the Court that the plaintiffs recover against the defendants the sum of two hundred and fifty and dollars ninety one and three fourth cents the debt in the declaration mentioned, also the further sum of eleven dollars thirty three cents being the interest on the aforesaid sum of two hundred & fifty one dollars and ninety one and three fourths cents at the vote of sixteen centum per annum from the first day of March 1835 upto this date making in all the sum of two hundred and sixty three dollars and twenty four cents - also the costs of suit.

Lemuel Feliston(?)
        vs   Debt - Came the the plaintiff by his attorney and the
Jacob K. Spooner   defendant being solemnly called came not but made default - It is therefore considered by the Court that the plaintiff recover against the defendant the sum of three hundred dollars the debt in in the plaintiffs declaration mentioned. also the further sum of six dollars, being the interest after the vote of six per centum per annum from the 10th day of August 1835 the time the debt in the declaration mentioned fell due upto this time on said debt making in all the sum of three hundred and six dollars - also the costs of suit.

P 213   James Shelton adm. &C.

vs

M. D. Redmond

Debt payment & set off - Came the parties by their attornies and a Jury of Good and lawful men to wit- Horace Oliver, William Reeves, Winston, Candles, Moses Reeves, Michael L. Uhls, Bartlet B. Uhls, Josiah Whitley, Sterling Jackson, Thomas I. Hubbard, Huey W. Glover, Cyrus W. Hazard and Daniel Driver who being elected tried and sworn the truth to speak upon the issue joined upon their oath do say, that they fine the issue in favour of plaintiff and they do assess the plaintiff damages by the detention of the debt in the declaration mentioned to seven dollars. It is therefore considered by the Court that the plaintiff recover against the deft. two hundred dollars and 9% cents the debt in the declaration mentioned and the P 214   damages aforesaid assed. no his cost about his suit in this befalf impended.

James Shelton administrator of the estate of A. Frith decd.

vs

William G. Langford

Case

Came the parties by their attorneys and thereupon came a Jury of good and lawful men, to wit, Horace Oliver, William Reeves, Winston Candler, Moses Reeves, Michael L. Uhles, and Bartlet B. Uhles, Josiah Whitley, Sterling Jackson, Henry W. Glover, Cyrus W. Hazard, Daniel Driver and Moses Reeves, who being elected tried and sworn the truth to speak upon the issue joined upon their oaths do say they find the issue in favour of the plaintiff and they do assess the plaintiff's damages occasioned by the non performance of the promises in the plaintiff's declaration mentioned to the sum of two hundred and fifty five dollars and thirty eight cents besides his costs. It is therefore considered by the court that the plaintiff recover against the defendant the aforesaid sum of two hundred and fifty dollars and thirty eight cents the damages aforesaid by the Jury aforesaid in manner and form aforesaid assessed and his costs by him about his suit in this behalf expended.

James Shelton administrator of the estate of Archd. Frith decd.

vs

John P. Langford

Case

Came the parties by their attornies and then came a Jury of good and lawful men to wit, Horace Oliver, William Reeves, Winston Candler, Moses Reeves, Michael L. Uhles, Bartlet B. Uhles, Josiah Whitley, Stirling Jackson, Henry W. Glover, Cyrus W. Hazard, Daniel Driver, and Moses Reeves, who being elected tried and sworn the truth to speak upon the issue Joined upon their oath do say they find the issue in favour of the plaintiff and they do assess the plaintiff's damage occasioned by the non performance of the promises in in the plaintiff's declaration mentioned to the sum of two hundred and fifty three dollars and twenty five cents besides his costs. It is therefore considered by the Court that the plaintiff recover against the deft. the aforesaid sum of two hundred and fifty three dollars and twenty five cents the damages aforesaid by the Jury aforesaid in manner and form aforesaid assessed and also the of suit.

P 215   State

vs

Samuel Yerger

Presentment for Drunkenness - Came the attorney Genl. for the state and and the defendant by his counsel David A. Crenshaw and the defendant by his attorney pleads guilty to the presentments and for his trial puts himself upon the mercy of the Court. It is therefore considered by the Court that the defendant "pay a fine of five dollars and the costs of this prosecution and David A. Crenshaw, Isaac Goodall and Henry B. McDonald here in open Court acknowledge themselves security for the fine and costs aforesaid and agree that execution may issue against them Jointly with the defendant for the fine and costs aforesaid.

John T. Stokes

vs

Willis Coggin

Debts - Came the parties by their attornies and thereupon came a Jury of good and lawful men to wit, Horace Oliver,

William Reeves, Winston B. Uhles, Josiah Whitley, Sterling Jackson, Henry W.
Glover, Cyrus W. Hazard, Daniel Driver and Moses Reeves, who being elected tried
and sworn the truth to speak upon the issue joined upon their oath do say they
find the issue in favour of the plaintiff and they do assess the plaintiffs
damages occasioned by the detention of the debt in the declaration mentioned to
the sum of seven dollars and fifteen cents besides his cost. It is therefore
considered by the Court that the plaintiff recover against the defendant the sum
of one hundred and thirty one dollars and eighty five cents the balance of the
debt in the declaration mentioned and the damages aforesaid assessed & the cost
of suit.

John T. Stokes
    vs
    Samuel Caplinger
Debt - Came the parties by their attornies and also a
Jury of good and lawful men to wit. Horace Oliver, William
Reeves, Winston Candler, Moses Reeves, Michael L. Uhles, Bartlet B. Uhles, Josiah
Whitley, Sterling Jackson, Henry W. Glover, Cyrus W. Hazard, Daniel Driver and
Moses Reeves, who being elected tried and sworn the truth to speak upon the issue
Joined upon their oath do say they find the issue in favour of the plaintiff, and
they do assess the plaintiffs damage occasioned by the detention of the debt in
the declaration mentioned to the sum of eight dollars and fifty cents besides
his costs. It is therefore considered by the Court that the plaintiff recover
against the defendant the sum of three hundred and forty dollars and ninety six
P 216 cents and the damages aforesaid assessed and the cost of suit.

Pearson Serrill
    vs
    Eliab Durham
Debt payment and Set off - Came the parties by their attornies, and then came a Jury of good and lawful men, to wit-
Horace Oliver, John L. Carter, William Reeves, Michael L. Uhles, Bartlet B. Uhles,
Josiah Whitley, Sterling Jackson, Cyrus W. Hazard, Henry W. Glover, Daniel Driver,
Winston Candler and Moses Reeves, who being elected tried and sworn the truth to
speak upon the issue Joined upon their oaths do say that they fine the issue in
favour of the plaintiff's and they do assess the Plaintiff's damage occasioned by
the detention of the debt in the declaration mentioned to thirty two dollars and
seven cents, besides his cost. It is therefore considered by the Court that the
plaintiff recover against the defendant hundred and sixty seven dollars and thirty
one cents the debt in the declaration mentioned and the damages afd. and the cost
of suit.

Mathew Watson, Robert Gibson
    vs
    Joel W. Hardwick
Debts payment & set off - Came the parties by
good and lawful men to wit, the same as in the
last proceeding cause, who being elected tried and sworn the truth to speak upon
the issues Joined upon their oaths do say that they fine the issues in favour of
the plaintiffs, and they do assess the plaintiffs damages occasioned by the detention of the debt in the declaration mentioned to ninety seven dollars and 64 cents
P 217 It is therefore considered by the Court that the plaintiffs recover against
the defendant five hundred and ninety one dollars and 95 cents the debt in the
declaration mentioned and the damages afd. assessed and the cost of suit.

Henry C. Jones
    vs
    Joel W. Hardwick
Debt payment & set off - Came the parties by their
attories, and the same Jury as in the preceeding cause,
who being elected tried and sworn the truth to speak upon the issues Joined, upon
their oaths do say that they fine the issues in favour of the plaintiffs and do
assess the plaintiffs damage occasioned by the detention of the debt in the declaration mentioned to Eighteen dollars besids cost. It is therefore considered by
the Court, that the Plaintiffs recover against the deft. four hundred dollars, the
debt in the declaration mentioned and his damage afd. assessed and the cost of suit.

James Shelton administrator of Archibald Frith ded.
    vs
    Robert M. Foster
Case non assump. (?)

Statute of limitation pay & set off. Came the parties by their attores and the same Jury as in the preceeding cause, who being elected tried and sworn the truth to speak upon the issues joined upon their oaths do say that they fine the issues in favour of the plaintiffs and do assess the plaintiffs damages occasioned by the non performances of the promises and assumptions in the plaintiffs declaration mention to thirteen dollars and forty two cents, besides his cost. It is therefore considered by the Court that the plaintiff's recover against the deft. the damages 218 afd. and his cost but his suit in this behalf expended.

Thomas Walker agent
vs   Came the parties by their attornies and on motion
Little B. Hughes admr.   this cause is continued by consent.

On motion and petition William Allen, is appointed Guardian ad litem for John Owen, of the minor Heirs of Dr. John Owen ded. to superintend the interest of said minor, in the division of the negroes, belonging to the estate of said John Owens ded. and on petition and motion, it is ordered by the Court, that John Gordon, Mathew Harper William Patterson, Exum Whitley and Wesley Haney are appointed Commissioners to divide the negroes belonging to the estate of said John Owen ded. between the Heirs of said John Owens ded. and make report to the next term of this Court.

Upon petition of Spencer Kelly administrator with the will annexed of Stephen Robinson deceased, supported by affidavit, and for reasons appearing to the satisfaction of the the Court, it is ordered that said administrator sell the negro slave Ben in the petition mentioned, at public auction, upon giving ten days previous days notice by advertisements on the Court house door in Carthage and in the town of Lancaster of the time and place of sale. The administrator will require one hundred dollars, part of the sum for which said negro may sell to be paid on the sale and the balance of the purchase money to be secured by bond & security at twelve months credit, and he will report to next Court &C.

P 219   The Commissioners appointed to settle with Jacob Fite administrator of H. G. Thrwett(?) ded. made their report which on motion is ordered to be recorded. and it is ordered, by the Court, that the administrator be allowed the sum of sixteen dollars as a compensation for his services out of said estate.

On motion Martha Fulks is appointed guardian to the minor Heirs of Jad Fulks ded. who came into Court together with Nathan Ward and Little B. Hughes her securities and entered into bond in the sum ten thousand dollars conditioned as the law directs.

The Grand Jury came into Court and made presentment against John Waters and Alexander Dillard for unlawfull gaming, ordered that capias issue, in both cases against said defts.

Be it remembered that this day came Jonathan Coggin and his wife Mamie (commonly called Polly) by their attornies and suggested to the worshipful Court of Pleas and Quarter sessions for said County that a paper writing purporting to - the last will and Testament of Nathaniel Corley their father was proven at a former Term of this Court and is filed in the record here, under the act of assembly and praying the Court to be permitted to contest the validity of said P 220 paper purporting to be such last will and Testament. and it appearing to the Court, that John Corley was appointed administrator of said Estate, with the bill amended, who comes into Court by attorny and says, that the paper writing purporting to be the last will and Testament of Nathaniel Corley is his last will and Testament which he prays may be inquired of by the Country. and the said Jonathan Coggin and his wife Mamie doth the like.

                                        John L. Brin &
                                        J. S. Yerger att's. for Deft.

The Grand Jury is discharge from further attendance at this Term, and proved as follows:

Solomon McMurry	8 days			
Judd Strother	8	do	and 4 Ferriages	
Henry Williams	8	do	4	do
Wommack Parper(?)	8	do		
William Shoemake	8	do	4	do
Zaddock B. Roberts	8	do	4	do
Neil Read	8	do		
John Reeves	8	do	4	do
James A. Scrugg	8	do	4	do
Taylor Whitley	8	do	4	do
Robert King	8	do	4	do
Lewis P. Hicks	8	do	4	do

Samuel D. McMurry one of the judges of the Qroran Court 8 days attendance.

Edward Evans excused from further attendance as a Juror at this Term and proved 8 day attendance & 4 Ferriages.

Jonathan Fuston a Juror, by the Court is also discharged proved 8 days and 4 Ferriages.

Isaac Smith discharged, as Juror, and proved 5 days attendance.

P 221   Caleb Read, a Juror is discharged proved 7 days attendance. Gregory Moore is discharged proved 8 days attendance

Simon P. Hughes and John Roe, acting under an order made at August Term, authorizing three to divide and set apart a list of hands to work under Wesley Motes overseer of the Road, made this report to Court, which is ordered to be recorded, and is as follows, to wit, B. W. Burford, John Moore, B. W. Harris, P. M. Wade, W. W. Wade, N. B. Burdine, T. T. Hamilton, T. I. Hubbard, J. H. Bedford, J. B. Burdine, S. Burdine and hands, S. M. Jones, N. Robison, B. Underwood, A. Walker, W. Willieford, A. Kilzer, M. Langford, Wm. Langford, Armstead Moore and hands, J. Trought, R. E. Campbell, Eli Atwood, James Cunningham and hands, James Sheltons hand at the quarter, James Harrison and hands, William Lawson, on motion it is ordered that said hands work under said overseer.

John R. Dougherty }
        vs   }   Attachment — Came the plaintiff by his attorney
Archer Robison   }   and the defendant Archer Robinson being solemnly
called came not but made default. It is therefore considered by the Court that the Plaintiff recover against the defendant one hundred and sixty two dollars thirty one and one fourth cents the debts in the declaration mentioned also the further sum of ten dollars seventeen and three fourth cents being the interest after the rate of six per cent per annum on the debts specified in the several writings obligatory declared on from the time they severally & respectively fell due upto this time, making in all the sum of one hundred and seventy two dollars and forty nine cents, also the costs of suit. And it is further ordered by the Court that the property levied on by the sheriff under the attachment in this cause be sold to satisfy the plaintiffs debt interest and costs aforesaid.

P 222   Court adjourns until tomorrow morning 9 oclock.

                                        Exum Whitley
                                        X. Goodall
                                        Henry B. McDonald

Friday morning Court met pursuant to adjournment present H. B. McDonald
                                        Exum Whitley and
                                        Isaac Goodall Esquires.

On motion Simon P. Hughes is appointed administrator of the Estate of George Rison ded. who came into Court and quallified together Andrew Payne, and Exum Whitley his securities and entered into bond in the sum of Eighteen hundred dollars conditioned as the law directs. Letters of administration is granted on said estate.

On motion Haney Hogg, Henry B. McDonald and John I. Bennett are appointed commissioners to settle with O. B. Hubbard administrator of Mathew W. Williams ded. and make report to next Court.

On motion William Owens Simon P. Hughes H. B. McDonald are appointed Commissioners to divide the negroes belonging to the State of Nathaniel W. Williams ded. and set off to Robert Williams and the widow of Nathaniel W. Williams ded. their respective shares & report to next Court.

P 223   James Shelton administrator of Arch'd. Frith ded.

vs   Case

Martin Moorefield

Came the parties by their attornies and a Jury of good and lawful men to wit Horace Oliver, William Reeves, Winston Candler, Moses Reeves, Stirling Jackson, Don C. Finly, Thomas T. Tyree, Spencer Kelly, Little B. Turner, Daniel Driver, Joshua L. Keelebrew(?), and Denson Fields who being elected tried and sworn the truth to speak upon issue joined upon their oaths do say that they find the issues and do assess the plaintiffs damages to five dollars & 33 cents in favour of the plaintiff. It is therefore considered by the Court - the Plaintiff recover against the defendant
P 224   the sum of seventy five dollars and thirty three cents the amount of the damages aforesaid assessed and his cost about his suite in this behalf expended.

Caplinger & Dougherty

vs   Case - Came the parties by their attorneys and

John T. Stokes   this cause is continued on the affidavit of the Plaintiff and on motion a commission is awarded the plaintiff to take the deposition of Daniel McCurley of Jackson County and of William Printis of Warren County on the Plaintiff's giving the defendant ten days notice of the time and place, and on motion it is further ordered that a commission by awarded the defendant to take the deposition de bene esse of John Terry on giving the plaintiff five days notice of the time and place of taking the same.

Simon P. Hughes

vs   Debt - Came the parties by their attornies and

Don C. Dixon, Andrew Payne   then came a Jury of good and lawful men to wit-
and John Baker administrator   Horace Oliver, William Reeves, Winston Candler,
of the estate of John Baker deed. Moses Reeves, Sterling Jackson, Don C. Finly, Thomas T. Tyree, Spencer Kelly, Little B. Turner, Daniel Driver, Joshua L. Kellabrew and Dinson Fields who being elected tried and sworn the truth to speak upon the issues Joined upon their oaths do say they find the issues in favour of the plaintiff, and they do assess the plaintiff's damages occasioned by the detention of the debt in the declaration mentioned to the sum of fourteen dollars and eight seven and one half cents besides his costs. It is thereupon considered by the Court that the plaintiff recover against the defendant two hundred and fifty dollars the debt in the declaration mentioned & his damages aforesaid amounting in the whole to the sum of two hundred and sixty four dollars and eight eight cents. also the cost of suit To be levied of the proper goods & chattels lands & tenements of said Don C, and Andrew, and of the goods & chattels of said intestate with hands of said administrator &C and at the request of the defendants by their atto. the plaintiff by his atto. agrees that execution shall not issue on this Judgment until the expiration of three months.

P 225   James Shelton administrator of the Estate of Archd. Frith ded.

vs   Debt

John & Jesse Allen

Came the parties by their attornies and a Jury of good and lawful men to wit
Horace Oliver, William Reeves, Winston Candles, Moses Reeves, Stirling Jackson,
Don C. Finly, Thomas T. Tyree, Spencer Kelly, Little B. Turner, Daniel Driver,
Joshua L. Keelebrew, and Denson Fields, who being elected tried and sworn the
truth to speak upon the issues joined upon their oaths do say they find the
issues in favour of the plaintiff and do assess his damage to five dollars and
seventy two cents & cost occasioned by the detention of the debt in the declaration mentioned. It is therefore considered by the Court that the plaintiff
recover against the defendant the sum of one Hundred and fifty two dollars 87½
cents The debt in the declaration mentioned, and his damages aforesaid and his
cost about his suit in this behalf expended.

Horace Oliver	Juror	9 days	& 4	Ferriages
William Penns	"	9 do	& 4	do
Moses Reeves	"	9 do	& 4	do
Stirling Jackson	"	9 do	& 4	dd
Winston Candler	"	8 "	4	

William Hart is permitted to pay a single Tax on the following property, 529¼
acres land, one third of two Town lots, also 4 Town Lots, one white and nine
Black polls for 1834 and the same for 1835 except one black poll less. The
taxes for said years amounting in all to twenty nine dollars, forty six cents
is paid into Court.

John Chambers
  vs   The death of Deft.
W. H. Jones & Jonathan Pickett
  Pickett having been suggested by consent the suit is recorded against Saml.
P. Howard & Andrew Pickett admr. &C & under a rule to plead & try at next term.

P 226 Archibald W. Overton came into Court and confess in favour of Huey B.
McDonald Chairman of Smith County Court a Judgment, one hundred and Eighty dollars
for Taxes from the year 1829 to 1834. It is therefore considered by the Court,
that Henry B. McDonald Chairman of Smith County Court, recover against said Archibald W. Overton, the sum of one hundred and Eighty dollars for the use and benefit
of Smith County and that said Judgment be stayed until August term of this Court,
and in case that the sd. Archibald W. Overton, to discharge or pay the same at
said August Term 1836 that Execution issue for the same together with all costs.

James Shelton administrator of Archd. Frith ded.
    vs   Case
  Crad(?) Penn admr. of George Penn
Came the parties by their attorney and a Jury of good and lawful men to wit -
Horace Oliver, William Reeves, Winston Candler, Moses Reeves, Stirling Jackson,
Don C. Finly Thomas T. Tyree, Spencer Kelly, Little B. Turner Daniel Driver,
Joshua L. Killebrew and Denson Fields well and truly to inquire of damages sus-
tained by the plaintiff in this case who being elected tried & sworn & the truth
to speak, upon their oaths do say that they assess his damages to seventy
three dollars fifty seven cents. It is thereupon considered by the Court that
the plaintiff recover against the defendant or administrator as aforesaid, seventy
three dollars fifty seven cents his damages aforesaid also the cost of suit. to
be levied of the goods & chattels of said George decd. in the good & chattels,
then the cost to be levied de bonis propras(?).

P 227 Polly Cornwell
    vs   Pet. in Dower
  The heirs of Francis Cornwell decd.
The Jurors summoned by the Sheriff under the ordered of a former term having made
their report. laying off and setting apart to said widow her dower pursuant to

the writ &c. It is ordered that the report of the jury aforesaid be recorded &c.

It being suggested to the Court that probably the taxes have not been paid on a tract of land & sundry town lots (for several years last past) owned by the heirs of Nathl. W. Williams and Thos Crutcher(?) and David Whiteside). It is ordered by the Court that the Clerk inquire into the matter, and if it shall satisfactorily appear that the taxes remain unpaid said clerk is authorized to receive a single tax on said tract of land and term (town?) lots for the years during which the taxes may remain unpaid as aforesaid, and the Clerk will report his proceedings under this order to the next term.

Court adjourns until tomorrow morning 9 oclock.

I. Goodall
Exum Whitley
Henry B. McDonald

Saturday morning 5 December 1835 Court met pursuant to adjournment, present the worshipful Henry B. McDonald,
Exum Whitley and
Isaac Goodall Esqrs. upon motion and for reasons appearing to the Court the order made at a former day of this term appointing separate commissioners to settle with Clerks, County Trustee &C are recorded and set aside - and it appearing that there was no appointment of commissioners at the regular Term pursuant to the provisions of the act of 1827. the Court to supply the omission appoint Henry Hogg and Andrew Allison commissioners of the County to settle with the Clerk & County trustee for the present year.

The Worshipful Justices issued their attendance at this term to wit:

Henry B. McDonald	Ten days
Exum Whitley	Ten days
Isaac Goodall	Two days
Joshua Sampson Constable	Twelve days

P 228   Court adjourned until Court in course &c.

Exum Whitley
I. Goodall
Henry B. McDonald.

INDEX to Smith County, TN Court Minutes

120

123

124

125

131

135

138

140